REVIVAL LIFESTYLE

IGNITING THE REVIVAL WITHIN

CHRISTINA ANDRIESE

DEDICATION

Jesus, after all You've given, my obedience is the least I can give.

Here are my loaves and fish. I adore You!

A REVIVALIST PLEDGE

We believe God the Father is a consuming fire, the Father of lights, and the source of all true revival.

We believe Christ is the resurrection and the life. He revives all He touches. He came to set fire to the Earth in a great kingdom revival. He is the sacred flame that ignites, the divine river that renews, the holy wine that intoxicates, the sovereign wind that blows where it pleases. He is the spirit that regenerates, sanctifies, illuminates, and revives. He is the Spirit of Divinity, pure, powerful, and miraculous. Where He is there is freedom and life.

We believe the word of God is alive and powerful. It is the divine revelation, the holy wisdom, it wounds and heals, kills and makes alive. It revives us, causing our hearts to burn. It instructs us with the fire of wisdom, giving us the mind of Christ. It is a lamp to our feet and a light to our path.

We believe prayer is the language of the heart that longs for revival. It is the incense of adoration, the cry of desperation, the shout of faith. It is effectual and powerful to bring heaven fire to Earth.

We believe the church is the community of Christ. It is the fireplace in which His fire burns, the keeper of the flame. It is the lampstand that shines. It is the light of the world. The church was birthed with fire on the day of Pentecost. That fire must never die but burn ever brighter until the coming of that great and glorious day. It cannot be contained. It must be spread until the entire world is aflame for Christ.

- Dr. Brian Simmons

CONTENTS

FOREWORD

Some people are mark makers. They're artisans. Craftsman. Simply good at what they do. Christina Andriese is a relational mark maker.

When I met Christina, I was coming out of what I refer to as the "Great Fire of 2016". It had been a season of deep, profound, life-altering loss for me, and the day that I limped into my first inner healing prayer session with her, I felt like I would never be the person that I had once imagined I could be. I believed I was irrevocably broken -- and yet something in me still hungered to know that I had a purpose. I needed to know there was still a call on my life. I wanted to heal, even if all I had faith for was just enough healing to get through the rest of my life with a smile on my face.

That day, Christina led me into the presence of Jesus. And in the end, it turned out I was right. I would never be the person that I had once imagined I could be. Instead, I would be something infinitely more beautiful, more powerful, and more precious: I would be a woman after Jesus' heart. After more than two hours of guided prayer and healing, Christina spoke life, family, hope, and friendship over me. She capped off a waterfall of poetic and prophetic words with her wonderful, shining smile and the phrase, "And Jesus wants you to know that you are not a hot mess!"

Since that day, she has continued to shape my walk and my life. She has been my friend, my confidant, my travel buddy, my fellow dreamer; she has strategized with me, risked with me, learned with me, and let me fail. If you have never had someone truly love you through failure, I bless you to receive that powerful experience. It will change you forever and is just one more way that Christina has shown me Jesus' face.

Once, when we were at a conference together, we were released to take a break. She stood up and looked around the room with a mischievous look on her face, and I instantly knew I was in for it. She glanced down at me, wiggled her eyebrows and grinned, saying, "Wanna take a risk?" That day, we ended up giving a powerful word of knowledge and healing to a girl sitting nearby, and I knew at that moment what it meant to give Jesus my 'yes'. It looked like following my friend into love.

And that's what this book is all about. It's an invitation from my dear (and your new) friend Christina into a full 'yes' to Jesus -- His lifestyle, His love, and His commission. I am praying and believing that you will be just as powerfully ignited in your life as I have been in mine, simply by learning from her example and catching the spark she carries.

She is, without a doubt, one of the most incredible teachers I have ever had the privilege to study under. She is compassionate and will always take the leap before encouraging you to do the same. Her time spent in the presence of the Lord is evident in her patience, her skill at asking brilliant questions, her effervescent charm, her buoyant praise, and her contagious love. As you read, I encourage you to hear the smile in her voice and the invitation in her heart -- I promise, you will find Jesus, Father God, and Holy Spirit celebrating at a feast table as you do.

With fiery hope, Tracy Meeker

INTRODUCTION

At fourteen years old, I visited a friend's family and their church plant in Arizona; I didn't understand all the connections or learn everyone's name. I don't really remember why I went. I was a freshman in high school and was invited to get away for the weekend. I had my bags packed before I had my parents' permission.

The family we were visiting and staying with were nice Christian folks. I don't remember anything from the trip other than our prayer time together before we left. The adults were praying for all of us and it was getting closer and closer to my turn. I wasn't uncomfortable or in a hurry. I had been a part of a Christian church my whole life, I sang on my youth group's worship team, and had been actively discipled since sixth grade through our schools' Christian Club. This situation was normal for me -- long as always -- but normal.

Knowing now how much I treasure prophetic words, I wish I would have written down everything that was spoken over my life that day. One thing I remember being said was that God would use me similarly to Smith Wigglesworth in two ways -- the healing anointing on his life and his great faith. I had never heard of Smith Wigglesworth before, though I remembered being fascinated by the summer "camp meetings" we had at our local pentecostal church. Each night they would bring in a man of God who would prophesy and pray for people to be healed. I remembered many people crying or screaming, testifying they had been touched by God.

I remembered being impressed and cynical -- but mostly curious.

Since the gifts of the spirit and manifestations of supernatural activity weren't a turnoff but more of an intriguing subject, I started to study the only revivalist I knew of -- you guessed it -- Smith Wigglesworth. Talk about next level. As I read books from the library (this was before the internet -- yes, I am that old) I learned the craziest things about this guy:

- He was a plumber by trade
- He was known as an angry man before he came to know Jesus in his later years
- He would hit people and tumors would come out of them
- He raised the dead many times

I needed to know more.

I had no problem believing that God could do miracles -- I had a hard time believing that God wanted to use broken people. But that year the Lord burned a hunger and thirst into me -- I was ravenous to learn about healing and miracles and to observe them with my own eyes.

I haven't always experienced that hunger.

There were many years -- almost a decade in my life -- when I wasn't hungry or searching for the truth about God's will. For those years, I didn't pursue or express a passion to heal, restore, save, and awaken the hearts of His people. I was figuring out how to avoid shame, what the purpose of my existence was, and how to pay my bills - but even then, the desire was always deep in my soul. I had a strong faith to believe in the miraculous grace of the Lord even if I wasn't consecrating myself to live in it.

Ten years and three kids later, that hidden hunger was reignited in a way that has remained burning in me since. Maybe the spark came out of boredom -- not that going to the park every day with toddlers isn't exhilarating. Maybe it came out of desperation -- I knew I needed the Lord to avoid screwing up my assignment as a mother and wife. But mostly it came out of a friendship. By that time in my life, I had experienced the Lord save me, heal me, set me free from shame and guilt and I was in love!

I'm now in my late thirties, and the reason I live is to love the Lord and to know Him more intimately, which accompanies a life of making Him known as well! Ten years ago, I never would have imagined the journey He has taken me on -- a journey filled with healing, a journey marked by deep faith, and a journey expressed in a revival of my own soul. This personal revival in my own life marked me internally and manifests externally -- people around me meet God, receive healing, get inspired to hope and dream, become renewed and made fully alive. Now I'm living in the middle of God's will and assignment for my life. It is a holy, terrifying, and amazing reality. Renewal -- awakening -- revival -- these aren't words that describe a singular experience I had or meeting I attended. They're words that have come to describe my daily living; the Lord has shown me that revival is a lifestyle.

I often imagine the revivalists of years past feeling the same way. It is the original design from God for all His kids to burn with passion for Him so that the fire of God on our lives brings both the atmosphere of heaven and Jesus' love to everyone that we come in contact with. The fire of God on our lives always leads to something miraculous and always starts with His love.

This reality looks different on all of us. His love is never-changing, and yet it manifests differently on and around each of His kids. From my years of studying revival history and being a follower of Jesus, I have found two things to be true: the Lord loves us all equally, and that alone qualifies us to have massive destinies that change the world.

Jesus' love has changed everything in my life! It's the place where revival has been birthed and sustained. It is the foundation for the gospel and everything after it. It is what keeps me continually alive in Him and saying 'yes'. His love is meant to be experienced when we say yes to salvation and every day after that. Revival renews the spiritual life and deepens our personal relationship with God. I choose to live in a continual revival that brings me face-to-face with the love and purposes of God for me and the world around me. It is from this place of renewal that I live.

I believe it is Jesus' very intention that we would be living flames of love -- living expressions of revival -- graced to carry His love which transforms nations all the days of our lives. It is my hope that as you read the pages of this book, your soul would be renewed again and your heart would be awakened for what can be -- that you will never again use the phrase, "We experienced a revival last night," or pray, "Lord would you bring us revival?"

It is my prayer that our time together will change your belief system from praying for a revival to being an authentic expression of it.

Thank you for traveling on this journey with me. Let's burn!

1

LOVE CHANGES EVERYTHING

I AM A LITTLE PENCIL IN THE HAND
OF A WRITING GOD WHO IS SENDING
A LOVE LETTER TO THE WORLD.
Mother Teresa

In the city of Jericho, there lived a very wealthy man named Zacchaeus, who was the supervisor over all the tax collectors. As Jesus made his way through the city, Zacchaeus was eager to see Jesus. He kept trying to get a look at Him, but the crowd around Jesus was massive. Zacchaeus was a very short man and couldn't see over the heads of the people. So he ran on ahead of everyone and climbed up a blossoming fig tree so he could get a glimpse of Jesus as He passed by.

When Jesus got to that place, He looked up into the tree and said, "Zacchaeus, hurry on down, for I am appointed to stay at your house today!" So, he scurried down the tree and came face-to-face with Jesus. As Jesus left to go with Zacchaeus, many in the crowd complained, "Look at this! Of all the people to have dinner with, he's going to eat in the house of a crook." Zacchaeus joyously welcomed Jesus and was amazed over his gracious visit to his home. Zacchaeus stood in front of the Lord and said, "Half of all that I own I will give to the poor. And Lord, if I have cheated anyone, I promise to pay back four times as much as I stole." Jesus said to him, "This shows that today life has come to you and your household, for you are a true son of Abraham. The Son of Man has come to seek out and to give life to those who are lost.

Luke 19:1-9 (TPT)

I LOVE how the Passion translation says Zacchaeus scurried down the tree and came face-to-face with Jesus. Zacchaeus was short, so Jesus would have had to bend down for this face-to-face encounter to happen. At that moment, the look of love, belonging, and compassion Zacchaeus encountered was so intense that his response was quick and full repentance. He instantly felt known and loved, and it changed everything.

In three years of public ministry, Jesus turned the world upside down. He challenged the status quo, making both friends and enemies. He was found guilty of treason against the government, and yet every person that came to Him sick, tormented, hungry, or marginalized was altered forever for the good. Both history and time were permanently changed, and He introduced people to another way of living. He flipped the script right in front of every observer and confronted even the "good guys'" view of life, humanity, and government. In essence, He taught us, "It all comes down to love."

This is why **John 3:16-17** is so powerful. In the Passion Translation, it reads, "For this is how much God loved the world — He gave His one and only, unique Son as a gift. So now everyone who believes in Him will never perish but experience everlasting life. God did not send His Son into the world to judge and condemn the world, but to be its Savior and rescue it!" He didn't come to bring a judgment against the world.

He came as a love gift to save it. The very nature of love changes things. This kind of love -- love that gives, saves, and rescues -- is Jesus' specialty. Jesus supernaturally fed thousands of people yet the next day they were hungry again. Jesus raised Lazarus and Jairus's daughter from the dead but eventually, they died again. His miracles changed circumstances for a time, but his love marked His followers and friends forever. The lasting significance of Jesus' ministry was not the miracles themselves but His great unchanging love.

THE WOMAN at the well from **John 4** met this love when she met Jesus. She was searching for a love that would rescue her from her pain, her isolation, her choices. She didn't know that kind of love actually existed and she didn't expect to come face-to-face with it one regular day as she was on her way to draw water.

Jesus arrived at the Samaritan village of Sychar, near the field that Jacob had given to his son, Joseph, long ago. Wearied by his long journey, He sat on the edge of Jacob's well. He sent His disciples into the village to buy food, for it was already afternoon. Soon a Samaritan woman came to draw water. Jesus said to her, "Give me a drink of water." Surprised, she said, "Why would a Jewish man ask a Samaritan woman for a drink of water?"

Jesus replied, "If you only knew who I am and the gift that God wants to give you—you'd ask me for a drink, and I would give to you living water." The woman replied, "But sir, you don't even have a bucket and this well is very deep. So where do you find this 'living water'? Do you really think that You are greater than our ancestor Jacob who dug this well and drank from it himself, along with his children and livestock?"

Jesus answered, "If you drink from Jacob's well you'll be thirsty again and again, but if anyone drinks the living water I give them, they will never thirst again and will be forever satisfied! For when you drink the water I give you it becomes a gushing fountain of the

Holy Spirit, springing up and flooding you with endless life!" The woman replied, "Let me drink that water so I'll never be thirsty again and won't have to come back here to draw water." Jesus said, "Go get your husband and bring him back here." "But I'm not married," the woman answered.

"That's true," Jesus said, "for you've been married five times and now you're living with a man who is not your husband. You have told the truth." The woman said, "You must be a prophet! So tell me this: Why do our fathers worship God here on this nearby mountain, but your people teach that Jerusalem is the place where we must worship. Which is right?"

Jesus responded, "Believe me, dear woman, the time has come when you won't worship the Father on a mountain nor in Jerusalem, but in your heart. Your people don't really know the One they worship. We Jews worship out of our experience, for it's from the Jews that salvation is made available. From here on, worshiping the Father will not be a matter of the right place but with the right heart. For God is a Spirit, and He longs to have sincere worshipers who worship and adore Him in the realm of the Spirit and in truth."

The woman said, "This is all so confusing, but I do know that the Anointed One is coming — the true Messiah. And when He comes, He will tell us everything we need to know." Jesus said to her, "You don't have to wait any longer, the Anointed One is here speaking with you — I am the One you're looking for."

At that moment the disciples returned and were stunned to see Jesus speaking with the Samaritan woman. Yet none of them dared to ask Him why or what they were discussing. All at once, the woman dropped her water jar and ran off to her village and told everyone, "Come and meet a man at the well who told me everything I've ever done! He could be the Anointed One we've been waiting for." Hearing this, the people came streaming out of the village to go see Jesus." **John 4:5-30 (TPT)**

We often refer to this woman as "the woman at the well". But early church history research reveals that she wasn't originally called by her position. (Thank God I am not "the woman in her bed" since that's where I choose to write.) Her name was Photini.[1] After her encounter with Jesus, she led her entire village to Christ. She was one of the early church's greatest apostles. Entire cities came to the Lord because of her. She led Emperor Nero's brother to Jesus and in response, Nero tried to kill her by putting her in a furnace for three days; she walked out unscathed. She was finally martyred with other women who were traveling with her spreading the love and good news of Jesus Christ.

The day she met Love Himself, she was forever marked, forever changed, and compelled to live differently. Love caused her to burn in a way that a fire in a furnace couldn't. The encounter with love that brought understanding, salvation, compassion, and wholeness to her motivated her to live differently. Love became her reason for changing the world. I propose to you that our encounters with Jesus should do the same. This is the byproduct of choosing love -- in love, we build trust with the Lord and He gives us opportunities to influence people around us. God knows He can trust you because in saying "yes" to love, you say "no" to ego, pride, status, and selfishness.

Apart from Jesus, none of us are worthy of the forgiveness, love, acceptance, and destiny God has given us **(Romans 3:23)**. It is in Jesus' worth and His death on the cross that my worth is no longer an issue. His love obliterated any need for personal qualifications! That same is true for all who believe in Him. It is this revelation and confidence in Jesus' death and resurrection that causes me to be confident in my own transformation and the transformation of all those who also believe.

LIKE ZACCHEAUS AND PHOTINI, once you have had an encounter with the love of God, you are a carrier of the love of God -- a carrier of revival! **Isaiah 12:3 (TPT)** says, "With triumphant joy you will drink deeply from the wells of Salvation." The word 'wells' can also be translated as 'fountains'. Through Christ, Christians are living wells of salvation; we are containers that bring the water of life to others. We are wells, carriers, messengers, ambassadors, and releasers of revival. Once we have said yes to salvation through faith we instantly become entrusted with the ministry of reconciliation which Paul writes to the Church in Corinth:

> And God has made all things new, and reconciled us to Himself, and given us the ministry of reconciling others to God. In other words, it was through the Anointed One that God was shepherding the world, not even keeping records of their transgressions, and He has entrusted to us the ministry of opening the door of reconciliation to God. We are ambassadors of the Anointed One who carry the message of Christ to the world, as though God were tenderly pleading with them directly through our lips. So we tenderly plead with you on Christ's behalf, "Turn back to God and be reconciled to Him." For God made the only one who did not know sin to become sin for us so that we who did not know righteousness might become the righteousness of God through our union with Him.

2 Corinthians 5:18-21 (TPT)

Or more familiar to us who have it memorized in the New International Translation: "God, who reconciled us to Himself through Christ and gave us the ministry of reconciliation: that God was reconciling the world to Himself in Christ, not counting people's sins against them. And He has committed to us the message of reconciliation. We are therefore Christ's ambassadors…"

What a mystery! What a privilege and a wonder!

I BELIEVE and hope to assure you that the Christian life was intended to look different from the Western conservative stereotypical picture of a person who attends weekend services and occasionally an outreach event. It looks different from a family that prioritizes church on the weekend but forgets to live like Jesus throughout the week. Author James Rutz argues in his book The Open Church that the successful organization of the church in 313 AD resulted in the degeneration of the church from a powerful family into passive spectators.[2]

Christianity is not a spectator sport. We were never intended to be a global audience. The intention of the Lord is that we all look more like Photini, a self-aware sinner transformed by the grace of Jesus -- conquered by love and compelled to respond. This love and saving grace is what empowers those of us who call ourselves Christians to be a united army of people on the mission of Jesus, to see the kingdom of darkness destroyed and the kingdom of heaven invade Earth.

INSERT LOVE HERE

YOU CAN NOT GIVE WITHOUT LOVING
AND YOU CAN NOT LOVE WITHOUT GIVING.
Amy Carmichael

MY SISTERS NATALIE and Andrea have taught me so much about love. We partner together in life in multiple ways -- developing my kids, pursuing each other's hearts, dreaming about the future, or simply running errands. We challenge each other to be great daughters, mothers, leaders, and lovers. It was in my childhood I heard the phrase, "Love is spelled T-I-M-E." It is as true now as it was then. It is always a good reminder as the demands on our time are ever-increasing and as a result, love can easily decrease in our lives.

I remember, a few years ago, Natalie and I were serving with an outreach team from a local church. We were hitting the pavement with our "Christian agenda." Doing what Jesus did, street ministry. We weren't window shopping, we were on a mission. We wanted to go back to the church with testimonies of healings and salvations. We had big faith and a skewed motivation. So the Lord used this day to teach me to let go of my desire for a story, even a miracle, and lean into the opportunity to love.

Street ministry is a great thing for every revivalist to experience. I don't love it or feel gifted in that type of outreach. However, I often lead teams just because I enjoy seeing people take risks and be activated in love. That being said, we need to be so careful that we don't turn people into projects or have an agenda as we go and tell others about Jesus. Agendas naturally violate and defile our love. Likewise, the days of bible-thumping debates, haughty displays of self-righteous living, and public expressions of our internal judgments need to end! Signs, wonders, miracles, and salvations are not a result of using those tools -- they are results of encountering a good God.

Jesus never made anyone or any group a project. He was never out in the city with a plan of pursuing social justice; He simply pursued love. He expects the same mindset in us and made that clear when He said, " For when you demonstrate the same love I have for you by loving one another, everyone will know that you're My true followers." **(John 13:35 TPT)**. We are to be known by our love. Revivalists aren't an advertisement for a product called Jesus; we are the evidence of a Loving God named Jesus.

Back to my story. While out on the streets, we came across some young kids who were dirty, smelly, and high. Our kind of people! We stopped to talk to them, just to let them know that they were not invisible. It became clear once we engaged in conversation with them that they were so high that anything we said might not be remembered or bear any weight in their hearts.

Insert love here.

Even if they didn't remember what we said, they could remember how they felt in our presence. My sister did something that I will never forget. She grabbed this one kid's hands and started playing hand-slapping games -- the kind that you do as a kid in the backseat of your car that inevitably leads to too much noise and your parents' eyebrows getting involved. As she did, I saw light fill this young man's eyes and they came into focus, his speech was no longer slurred. He sobered up for a few minutes as he encountered a moment in time with love. We were witnessing a miracle as we watched what love could do!

The Lord started to show me a vision of this stoned teenager as a young child in his home. He was a sweet boy full of adventure and wonder. He was laughing and holding his dad's hands as they walked and talked together. They had a beautiful connection. I could see him receiving so much love from his family through physical touch, care, meals. He was a beloved son. Suddenly the Lord showed me what He was doing! He was touching this young man! He was using this current act of love and affection to sober him up to what he was longing for, but not currently experiencing. He was miraculously physically sobered, but also spiritually sobered. The Lord was bringing awareness to his heart of what he really wanted. He wasn't going to find it in a drug, or on the streets.

Love must be more about conversations than conversions so that we can recognize a "moment" when it arrives. Those moments of love -- where those around us feel God's heart, not our agendas -- are real expressions of us living into our destiny as revivalists and ministering to those around us. A moment of love can be powerful enough to bring dignity, heal a need, and transform a life. This is what Jesus brought to Zacchaeus and Photini. This is how we can bring Jesus to others.

I want to activate you to carry the love of Jesus so that His love can be our purpose and motivation to change the world and share the gospel. I want to champion you to walk in the spirit of awakening and renewal that invites your heart to know Him, see Him, and hear Him continually. The same spirit which set revival ablaze in me is within you! And you don't need a church service, a prophetic word, a white tent, or a natural disaster to tell you otherwise.

I was recently teaching a class at my church about this and I presented this question: "If revival was dependent on love, how close do you think we are in seeing it?" It turned into a great discussion because many people have a view of revival that is different from my own. Recall Jesus' words, "Your love for one another will prove to the world that you are my disciples" **(John 13:35 NLT)**. Is it possible that we can and have the grace, the ability to maintain a good reputation for love?

Some generations and cultures have struggled with this more than others -- at times the Bride of Christ has had a bit of an identity crisis! We've emphasized Jesus' words about taking the kingdom by force **(Matthew 11:12)** and deemphasized His words about love **(John 13:35)**. But I wonder, if our generation got love right -- if we lived with a burning passion to see how far love would take us while also living with the constant awareness of the goodness of God, His plan for us and His family -- I wonder what would be different. Wondering doesn't keep me sedentary; wonder promotes action in my heart and this is the journey I am on with you.

Let's keep reading!

Let's keep loving!

Let's keep burning!

LET ME HEAR YOUR VOICE -- THAT IS MY PRAYER.
I AM WILLING BEYOND ALL MY EXPRESSION TO HEAR YOU,
TO PERCEIVE YOU, TO BE THRILLED WITH YOUR PRESENCE.
Oswald Chambers

2

YOU ARE GOD'S HAPPY THOUGHT

WORKING FOR LOVE IS A CURSE.
WORKING FROM LOVE IS A MINISTRY.
Kris Vallotton

REMEMBERING what we read in **2 Corinthians 5:19**, "For God was in Christ, reconciling the world to Himself, no longer counting people's sins against them..." Let's shift our gaze from being face-to-face with Jesus to being face-to-face with His Dad. This verse reveals to the world that it wasn't just Jesus' idea to die for us but it actually was His Father's as well! This is where many followers of Jesus get stuck. We connect to Jesus; He was a man, He was a good teacher, and a leader so we can relate to Him. It can be harder for some of us to translate the connection or acceptance of Jesus to His Father.

If we are believing something about Jesus' goodness that we don't believe about Father God's goodness, we are believing a lie. A partial truth is a full lie. As a parent, if my kid kinda lies to me, they don't receive a partial discipline, they get a full discipline. As a parent, I recognize they have an integrity issue that needs redemption. It's not the amount of lie in the lie, it's the fact that they lied that invites my love through discipline! Make sense? Believing that it was solely Jesus' idea to save humanity from sin and death is a lie. It was Father God's idea, and I believe it cost the Father something tremendous. God was in Christ bringing us to Himself.

Bill Johnson, a senior leader and pastor at Bethel Church in Redding, California, is quoted often for saying, "Jesus Christ is perfect theology." This means, whatever we believe about God that we don't see in Jesus' life, character, teaching, and choices is not true. For example -- when we believe that we are loved by Jesus but not loved by Father God we have a perversion of God's character and a perversion of His Love. A perversion is a different version of the truth (or a partial truth). It is the perversion of truth that holds us back from what is true and safe. Full truth found in Christ Jesus, His Father, and His Spirit is what sets us free **(John 8:32)**. Let me illustrate this with a story.

IN THE EARLY 1900S, there was a well-known affluent Italian doctor who lived in a small town called Gorizia. He had two daughters that he loved very much. From the time they were young, he taught them everything he knew about medicine, the human body, and how to own a business. He also taught them virtues like compassion and mercy. He was respected in their town and everyone wanted to work for him. His reputation as a surgeon was as famous as his reputation as a father. Their family was known in their town not just for their money and the hospital which the good doctor ran but for their kindness and generosity. The good doctor and his daughters were often seen in the streets talking with random people and helping anyone they saw in need.

Every summer the good doctor would take time off of work so they could travel together, build memories, and serve the poor. As the girls grew, they enjoyed this time with their father and also became accustomed to their lifestyle. They both felt an expectation to be like their dad -- smart, devoted to others, and well-versed in medicine.

The good doctor was an extremely hard worker. He sent both his girls to a private school and then to college to practice medicine. His greatest dream was that they would take over his practice one day and that they would be able to find great fulfillment in service to people who were wounded, broken, and sick.

The oldest daughter graduated with her degree in medicine a year early and went right into the medical field, taking on many of her father's patients in the hospital. It was a turbulent time as the Great War was being fought and Italy was a member of the triple alliance with Austria-Hungary and Germany. The good doctor was often busy in meetings; at any moment their armies could be asked to join their allies in fighting the Great War. He spent considerable time trying to ensure Italy did not join the fight.

One summer, the last summer before the youngest daughter graduated from medical school, they were preparing to take their summer trip together like always. The father took time off, the oldest daughter slowed down and took her holiday, but then the youngest daughter said she wasn't going to go. She told her father that instead, she wanted to find herself -- that he was suffocating her with all the opportunities he was giving her. "It is too much pressure to be like you!" She accused him, "I just want to be normal!" She didn't want to be known by her family name -- it was too high profile. She didn't want the responsibility that came with being her father's daughter.

While observing the interaction between her baby sister and father, the oldest daughter thought her sister was acting immature and ridiculous. She tried to interrupt, to fight for their family, to convince her sister that their life and the expectations that came with it really weren't that bad. After unsuccessfully trying to convince her to go with them she hardened her heart, turned her back, and walked out of the room.

The father was heartbroken. He loved both his daughters. He didn't want to lose either of them. Being a good doctor and a good father, he also knew he couldn't control them, and that love demanded a response. After much thought, he decided the only just thing, the only fair thing to do, was to divide everything he owned between his girls. He went to the bank, split up his investments, and turned over the title to his house and practice to both his daughters. He came back home and gave half of what he owned to his youngest daughter who haughtily took it and left.

No thank you.

No goodbye.

No promise of return.

Some time passed. It was the year 1915, and despite the good doctor's efforts Italy ended up fighting in the first of many battles. So close to the front lines of battle, the good doctor and his oldest daughter labored 20 hours a day providing aid to thousands of civilians who were displaced due to the war. Most of them were dying from malnutrition and illness.

The dream in the good doctor's heart came to be as his oldest followed in his footsteps. She traveled to different refugee camps helping as many people as she could. Sleeping only a few hours a day in efforts to save her country from destruction, she often thought of her baby sister and would be filled with bitterness and anger. So, she chose to work even harder. When gentlemen would want to date her, she would refuse, thinking her father wouldn't approve. She set herself to work and to serve as many civilians, refugees, and soldiers as she could just like her father taught her. One battle turned into two, turned into three, and before they knew it three years had passed and Italy was still at war.

The good doctor lost track of his baby girl, who ran as far away from him as she could. She didn't just run from him but from the city that knew her well and the expectations that she felt came with being known. She ran from her education both in college and compassion. Instead of fostering kindness, she turned spiteful. Having to watch her own back as she partied at discos and bars, she turned into an angry insecure woman who often instigated fights so she could feel better about herself. After she lost much of her money, she turned to enticing soldiers to sleep with her by promising her affection but stealing their purity and wealth. Instead of being gracious, she was malicious. Instead of assisting the broken, she destroyed anyone who crossed her path.

Finally, the youngest daughter ran out of money and found herself rejected by everyone she had built her life with. She had tricked and betrayed so many men she was in fear for her life. She couldn't even sell her body for food since she had contracted hepatitis from her loose living. She was starving to death when she came to her senses and thought to herself, "Even the janitors working in my dad's hospital are living better than I am. What am I doing here?" But could she ever go back, she wondered? She believed she had no right to be her father's daughter but thought, "Maybe he will let me wash the dirty linens in the hospital, maybe even sweep the floors in the middle of the night when no one was around."

She was terrified to make the journey home -- to see the faces she used to play with at the park, the students she studied with, her father's employees she worked with, her sister she laughed with, her father she was safe with. There was no way she would be welcomed back, but it was try or die in the street, discarded, with no dignity like the wounded enemy soldiers she now stepped over. She had no other choice. So, she started to walk. The journey was hard because she was so sick. It took her longer than she had anticipated and she was so weak from traveling she had a hard time seeing clearly. She would pause often to catch her breath, wipe her eyes, and entertain thoughts about turning back.

It was during one of these breaks she heard a familiar voice shouting in the distance, calling her by name. Unable to make out the figure that was coming closer and closer and thinking she was hallucinating, she fell on her knees. Within moments, she was scooped up into the arms of her father. The moment she was in his arms, she was kissed and met with a look of tender love. The love was overwhelming. She was so ashamed of her appearance that she pulled away and fell to the ground in front of him. Exhausted and humbled, she couldn't look him in the eye or call him daddy. She said to him, "Esteemed Dr. Moretti, I know I shouldn't be here. I've done such horrible--" and he stopped her. He wouldn't let her finish her sentence as she tried to repent.

He picked her up like he used to when she was a young girl, rubbed her head, kissed her dirty face, and told her it didn't matter anymore. She looked up at him with tears streaming down her face. She said, "I am unworthy to be called your daughter." He interrupted her again and said, with tears streaming down his face, "I am so happy you came back!" He gave her the keys to the house and instructed her to shower and get dressed. "Tonight we will celebrate your return!" He told her, "We will eat, drink, and share stories! We will pick up where we left off and build memories with one another once again! But first I must go get your sister and tell her the good news!"

Elated, he drove off to tell the good news to his first-born daughter! She was tending to a new round of wounded warriors. When he found her, she was rushing in between surgeries and executing orders to her nurses. Rushing around like a madwoman, she didn't make eye contact with him when he came in, she was too busy to notice his presence. Finally, he got her attention and shared the good news with her. The father looked at her and said, "You'll never believe it! Your sister has returned!! Come home with me. Leave your work behind! I have already told our friends to come over! We are going to have a huge celebration."

The daughter pulled out of her father's arms, flooded with all the thoughts of what she had given up throughout the years. Her face instantly turned red as she was filled with contempt for her sister.

She looked up at her father and saw a look in his eyes of deep love. This infuriated her even more and she responded back to him, "Dad, are you kidding me? You want me to walk away from my work -- to celebrate my sister who has no regard for me, or you, or our people? She has been out there having a good old time, wasting away your money, probably behaving like a fool, shaming our family's name... I've been here for years doing everything you've taught me. There is no way I am going to celebrate her. All these years I've worked, learned, and sacrificed my own happiness, I've never even asked you for anything!"

Suddenly she was filled with jealousy over her sister! She wondered if she wasted years of hard work and devotion -- wondered why she stayed and what she gained for her servitude.

Her father interrupted her thoughts by handing her an old piece of paper. Still furious she opened it; it was the title to their home and the hospital. She noticed her name was on it and it was dated four years ago. He pulled her chin so her eyes met his and said, "All these years you have stayed by my side, you've learned well what I do, but you haven't learned why I do it. All this that we have been building together is for you to enjoy. It belongs to you. I always intended it to be a gift out of my love, not a reward for your work. My love for you and your sister has no cost or expectation attached to it. So then it is right that we celebrate your sister's return. She was far from my love and now she is back!"

We normally hear this story, told by Jesus and recorded in Luke 15, a little bit differently. Hopefully, this retelling sheds new light on the power and full truth found in the parable. The heading in our Bibles is often "The Prodigal Son". As we read it, we tend to frame it as a story about evangelism due to the perspective of the lost son. But what about the role of the son that stayed? What about the role of the Father? Are they just supporting characters? Just names added at the end of the credits that say "also starring a good dad and a tired son"?

Prodigal means "lavish, too-generous, over-generous, or extravagant". As I read the scriptures, I read a story where the main character is the prodigal father rather than a lost son or an overworked son. In my humble opinion, it might be more appropriate to entitle this parable "the extravagant father with two orphan sons". Both of the sons were acting like orphans because of what they believed about their father and their position in their family. You could say the distortions they believed about their father effectively rendered them to be orphans.

If a perversion is a different version of the truth, then distortion is the act of twisting or altering something out of its true, natural, or original state. Distortions about God happen when we sin, refuse to process hurt and pain, embrace a hurried lifestyle or shame, or partner with pride and unforgiveness (to name a few). Sometimes we have distorted views about God because of bad teaching or experiences with an absent earthly father.

In the parable, the younger son behaved like an orphan through his immaturity, entitlement, and stupidity. He saw his father as a sugar daddy. The elder son behaved like an orphan through his self-righteousness, performance, and religious tendencies. He despised his own brother and separated himself from the family through judgment, bitterness, compulsive work, busyness, and criticism. He saw his father as a harsh taskmaster; he was a son, but he saw himself as the hired help.

It took me a few years to tap into the revelation of Father God from **Luke 15**. I knew it in my mind that God was good, but I was just more comfortable with Jesus than I was with the guy I saw in my imagination on a throne in heaven with a bit of a stern look on His face. It wasn't that I had daddy issues growing up, I just couldn't connect to His goodness and love in my life. I was grateful for Him but preferred a safe, holy distance. Does that sound familiar at all?

Father God was patient with me. He is patient with all His kids. Interestingly, the Prodigal Father in the parable didn't respond to the behavior of either of the kids; he responded from the love that was in his own heart for them. This is a love that transcends a church, a religion, culture, or a lie (whether a perversion or a distortion). It's the love of a Father for His family. God has not changed His mind about us. In **John 15:9 (NIV)**, Jesus says "As the Father has loved me, so have I loved you." I haven't read anything that has said otherwise. The Bible also says:

> "Jesus' God-given destiny was to be the sacrifice to take away sins, and now He is our mercy seat because of His death on the cross. We come to Him for mercy, for God has made a provision for us to be forgiven by faith in the sacred blood of Jesus. This is the perfect demonstration of God's justice, because until now, He had been so patient — holding back His justice out of His tolerance for us. So He covered over the sins of those who lived prior to Jesus' sacrifice. And when the season of tolerance came to an end, there was only one possible way for God to give away His righteousness and still be true to both His justice and His mercy — to offer up His own Son. So now, because we stand on the faithfulness of Jesus, God declares us righteous in his eyes!" **Romans 3:25-26 (TPT)**

Our righteous God wanted His kids so intensely, He found a way to be both just and merciful by offering up His Son and getting us in the exchange. It would do us much good to understand we are loved by both Jesus and Father God. It isn't as if Jesus is the nice parent and God is the mean one. Or as Graham Cooke so hilariously says it, "God is not schizophrenic." Every time Jesus Christ was face-to-face with someone while He was on Earth, God was also looking with His eyes of love at that person. An encounter with love comes with Jesus' and God's desire. Revelation of His love is the gateway, the portal where we become revived in our souls so we can bring the source of true revival everywhere we go. It is not just Jesus' desire for there to be revival fires burning everywhere on the Earth -- it is also Father God's heart.

I have acted like both the lost son and the self-righteous son from **Luke 15**. There have been many times I have run from my destiny, and many times I have hustled for my Father. I have been jealous of others who wasted time and allowed regret to keep me from returning home.

Shame keeps us from looking into the tender gaze of Jesus' eyes; from making eye contact and being face-to-face!

I'm wondering as you are reading if you can relate?

The extent that we can believe the truth about who God is in our lives and what He did through His son will affect the way we burn for Him all our days. The perversion of truth will make a case for working to earn His love. Another perversion would be never receiving it because we aren't worthy of it. The real version is simple, He has created us to be His and we have the choice to live surrounded by His love. In fact, this is the way to live out our relationship with Him and change the world: to position ourselves in the middle of His love and do whatever He says. This is how revival is possible as a lifestyle without burnout, without fear, without pride. It's the secret to ending our race well, never moving away from the love of God in Christ Jesus. If Paul can do it, that means there is grace; the empowering presence of Jesus Christ makes it possible for all of us to finish well too! I don't know about you, but I want to be able to say something similar to what he wrote to his spiritual son in **2 Timothy 4:7 (NIV)**, "I have fought the good fight, I have finished the race, I have kept the faith."

Years ago, I was spending time with the Lord in silence. In a vision in my mind, (some people refer to this as a faith visualization), I saw myself running. I was running as hard as I could and eventually arrived at a palace. I knew in my spirit that Father God was inside. I slowed to a walk since it is inappropriate to run in a palace and was heartbroken to see a line of people waiting to have a conversation with Him. I walked the length of the line and eventually hid behind these larger thick red curtains. I kept looking around trying to find a way to the front, a better view, or gap in the line where I could cut in.

I couldn't see Father God or hear what He was saying to His children. I was frustrated so I stopped peeping and joined the end of the horrific line. I decided it was better to wait than not see Him at all. Before I knew it, I hadn't waited long at all, I heard a commotion and saw the Holy Spirit run towards me. He passed up everyone else to embrace me. As I buried my face into Him, I heard Him whisper, "We are healing your orphan spirit."

In my rational mind, I thought about the lack of identity an orphan has -- the confusion, the fear, the feeling of not having enough, of not being enough, and of not having the stability of belonging in a family. I instantly knew in my spirit I was believing a perversion about my identity as a child of God. Since my belief system was built on a lie, the Lord knew I needed to be healed. I watched, in this vision, as the Holy Spirit took my hand and brought me before Father God in heaven. I climbed onto His lap and observed around me as Father God turned His face towards mine. He looked tenderly at me and I heard Him say, "Nothing is withheld from the ones I love. You are my happy thought."

It had been a while since I watched the movie Hook, yet the language connected to my soul. I was God's happy thought! "Shoot, what else needed to be said?" I thought to myself. It was as if the Lord was making new glasses for me in real-time -- new lenses forged from faith, confidence, and identity. As He put them on me, I saw differently! It all happened in my spirit and this vision only lasted a few seconds. It was an encounter I had with Father God that led to a new way of seeing and receiving His love. I was His happy thought and all lies or perversions about my position, works, or worth in Christ that opposed truth disappeared. I had experienced a moment in time with His love and it changed everything; and I was ready for what was next.

HE SAID, "LOVE... AS I HAVE LOVED YOU."
WE CANNOT LOVE TOO MUCH.
Amy Carmichael

3

THE LOOK OF LOVE

TO LOVE AT ALL IS TO BE VULNERABLE.
LOVE ANYTHING AND YOUR HEART WILL
BE WRUNG AND POSSIBLY BROKEN.
C.S. Lewis

I WISH we were in a room together, sojourning face-to-face into the heart of God as a group. I wouldn't be your teacher -- I would be an instigator. I would be asking you all the questions that no one has a concrete answer to that would inspire critical thinking and deep growth in the Lord. (At least that's my goal). I wish I could ask you this question: when you hear the word 'revival', what do you think of? What does it mean to you? Do you think it's a meeting? An experience? Or a once in a lifetime opportunity? Do you associate any people with the word revival? You'll get to hear what I think as you keep reading, and I think it's only fair I take your thoughts into consideration as well!

I enjoy studying church history. I've been fascinated with biographies for as long as I can remember -- even in elementary school, I was always reading about people like Hellen Keller, Louis Braille, and Fredrick Douglas. Anyone who specifically overcame impossible situations attracts my attention. As I aged, I added Christian leaders to my reading list -- whether they were church leaders, political leaders, or outcasts, I was insatiable. I devoured biographies about Corrie Ten Boom, Wiliam Wilberforce, and Jim Elliot; I still can't get enough! I encourage my kids to read them too!

Each of these people is a revivalist in their own way; each one of them lived out their relationship with Jesus in such a way they were ignited with a passion that changed the world and left an indelible mark:

- Ammie Semple McPherson wrote operas, pioneered Christian television, and fed millions of people in the middle of the Great Depression.
- Martin Luther relentlessly pursued truth and crafted his 95 issues with the Church which led to a global reformation.
- Kathryn Kulman operating out of her eccentricities and pure connection with the Holy Spirit brought people into mystical encounters with the Lord.
- John G. Lake and Smith Wigglesworth carried healing anointings and great faith which resulted in incredible miracles.
- Hudson Taylor, Billy Graham, and Reinhard Bonnke led millions of people to salvation in Jesus Christ.
- George Muller cared for thousands of orphans and never publicly or privately asked anyone for financial assistance or help.
- William Wilberforce and Abraham Lincoln were politicians and leaders of movements that ended the legalization of slavery.

#goals

Can I just say that is the short list?! There are hundreds more that I didn't mention, and hundreds more whose stories are still being written; you, my friend, are one of those!

As I studied and compared their lives, I saw many similarities and many differences. Each revivalist met Jesus under different circumstances, had a unique family life, and carried a burning passion for the Lord. They all had profound encounters with Jesus and lived out of their devotion to Him. They were all confident, bold, and had great faith. Some ended their ministries or professions with their integrity and some didn't. Some had secret struggles and some led lives of holiness. Some were married and some weren't. Their zeal manifested differently in each of their lives, and I learned that a person can be zealous and not motivated by love. I also learned that these were "normal" men and women similar to the disciples Jesus chose when He was on Earth. I also observed that there is no formula for being called by God, but there is one common denominator: they were all humans that Jesus loved fiercely!

LET'S look at what love requires from scripture:

"As Jesus started on his way, a man came running up to Him. Kneeling down in front of Him, he cried out, "Good Teacher, what one thing am I required to do to gain eternal life?" Jesus responded, "Why do you call Me good? Only God is truly good. You already know the commandments: 'Do not murder, do not commit adultery, do not steal, do not give a false testimony, do not cheat, and honor your father and mother.'" The man said to Jesus, "Teacher, I have carefully obeyed these laws since my youth."

Jesus fixed his gaze upon the man, with tender love, and said to him, "Yet there is still one thing in you lacking. Go, sell all that you have and give the money to the poor. Then all of your treasure will be in heaven. After you've done this, come back and walk with Me."

Completely shocked by Jesus' answer, he turned and walked away very sad, for he was extremely rich." **Mark 10:17-21 (TPT)**

This young man was given a special invitation: to follow Jesus. He could have been the thirteenth disciple, but he couldn't live without his money. It wasn't that he didn't know how to love, he just didn't know how to love the right thing. He was accustomed to a lifestyle that was familiar and comfortable, possibly even predictable and safe. He knew what to expect, how to perform, and be self-sustained. He developed patterns to predict his success. He embraced rules and habits and mastered external performance. But he did not know how to rely on someone else. He was unfamiliar with vulnerability and dependency so he couldn't say yes to follow Jesus.

I love the description in verse 21: "Jesus fixed his gaze upon the man, and with tender love spoke to Him." I know the look of tender love from Jesus. I've seen it many times. Love precedes the 'yes' in our hearts. Love comes before our surrender. Like we said in the last chapter, love is the gateway, the portal; our introduction to knowing Jesus. Love is our reference point and our purpose. Love is where holiness becomes attractive and develops in our lives.

LEAVE IT ALL IN THE HANDS THAT WERE WOUNDED FOR YOU.
Elizabeth Elliot

I WASN'T the kind of kid that had a soft heart or pliable nature. I've always been stubborn, strong-willed, thick-skulled, and persistent. It took me years to learn intimacy. When I was young, I learned that being vulnerable was risky, so shutting off and shutting people out was the safest thing to do. This happens to many of us. That is why many people live without deep connections, prefer to have sex with random people, or believe they are better off by themselves. Often, it takes years of counseling for people to connect the dots. I have never met anyone who consciously decided at a young age, they were going to be unhappy or they were better off without love. That is a response born out of a need for self-protection, from broken trust, or experiencing trauma and loss. It also happens when we make vows in our hearts or with our mouths like, "I will never love again".

I GREW up in a Christian home with first-generation Christian parents who did a great job teaching me and my siblings about Jesus. I went to church on Sunday mornings, Vacation Bible School at least three times a summer, and spent my youth days playing chubby bunny at Bible study. I was deeply involved in my youth group because it seemed like one of the only acceptable activities for me to participate in, per my parents' preference. Unfortunately, this involvement didn't benefit me the way my parents were hoping; I attended meeting after meeting and ended up viewing Christianity as a boring, repetitive, behavioral interaction rather than a relationship.

I knew of God, but I didn't know His heart. I loved Jesus, but I didn't know how to allow Him to love me, so as I aged and experienced life I spent more time living in shame than living as one who is loved. As a result, I became extremely calloused, responsible, and independent. Because vulnerability was risky, I was always guarded and surface-level with everyone. I struggled to follow anyone's lead -- including God's. I can relate to our rich young ruler very well.

I would say I trusted the Lord and meant it, but that came from a place of performance, not internal peace. It appeared as if I knew His word and it looked like I had a relationship with Him, but it turned out I was pretty good at performing and acting. So much so that I decided to pursue a career on the stage. In college, I studied music as a Vocal Performance Major. I dreamed of traveling the world as one of America's most talented leading lyric sopranos. I envisioned performing operas by day and then sneaking into jazz bars late in the evening to enjoy myself in a smoky, relaxed, less-sophisticated environment. I gave a lot to that dream: hours of practice, stressful college semesters. I even became extremely anorexic, so I could look and sing the part. That dream didn't come to be. I should have known that any dream with the goal of performance would have an expiration date.

After college didn't work out, my identity was destroyed. Everything I had worked so hard to accomplish was thrown in the trash. The tools I learned as a kid -- like hard work, self-reliance, and isolation -- didn't help me. So naturally, I looked for acceptance and a rebound. This launched me into an extremely dysfunctional relationship, where I exchanged my old tools for a set of new ones: victimization, cowardice, fear, and anxiety, all while shame slowly stole my dreams and peace.

It's hard to imagine someone as strong-willed and independent as I was, willfully involved in a relationship with physical and emotional abuse. But that's exactly where I found myself. I learned first-hand how someone who hasn't experienced peace in such a long time will justify chaos in their life as if they didn't miss peace at all. Being manipulated and living in fear day after day bred more and more shame. I became so miserable, so isolated from people that loved me, that even in the face of death, I didn't have a will to live.

But then I had something to live for. I became pregnant with my daughter. Survival rose up in me, and I finally grew desperate… for her sake. Desperation led me to stand up for myself and walk away from the situation as well as the fear and shame I had agreed to live in. To my surprise, leaving him wasn't the end of my life as he had threatened. It was just the beginning.

Painfully broke with a new baby, mortgage payments, and worthless tools -- everything about life at that time seemed so unhealthy and desperate. But I knew that being alive was in itself a miracle. I also realized that all the ways of operating or performing I had tried in the past didn't and would never work. So, my heart was primed and ready to receive the tender look of love from Jesus. I remember vividly the night Holy Spirit spoke 2 Corinthians 5:17 over me, telling me that old things had passed away, and He was making me a new creation. That meant I didn't have to perform anymore. That meant I could lean on Him -- that I did not have to do everything on my own. That meant freedom to dream again about the life I wanted to live and the kinds of things I wanted to do. Instead of giving myself to fear and captivity, I could give myself to love and freedom.

It was not long after this Jesus showed me how good He is at exchanging His beauty for our shame. Ian and I started dating and he treated both me and Aria with such dignity and love; it was like breathing for the first time. We were engaged and married within two years of meeting each other. And since then, I have experienced the transformation of living as a servant of God to having a friendship with Him. Jesus has replaced all my bad tools for good ones -- freedom, love, grace, authority, joy, and servanthood. There's no need to perform or pretend because love is so liberating.

Once the Lord healed me, I learned the value of intimacy and every one of my relationships changed; it started with my relationship with the Lord, then trickling down to my relationship with my parents, siblings, friends, kids, and husband. I've learned to look back into the eyes of Jesus without pulling away and embrace his tender love in the soil of my heart which is now soft. Truly embracing His love -- choosing to be vulnerable with Him -- felt like a risk in the beginning. The rich young ruler couldn't do it. It took me years to be able to do it. I pray my kids give in to Him and His love at a young age! Maybe even as you are reading this you feel the Holy Spirit whispering for you to lean in, to look into His eyes, to choose the fullness of His tender love right now. Do it. Put the book down and do it. Don't look away! Allow His love to change everything for YOU!

OUR LIVES, fully lived, are actualized in Christ. Saying yes to Him when we have millions of occasions to say yes to other things is the greatest choice we could ever make. Since a full "yes" turns into a life of consecrated passion and influence, it is the greatest demonstration of the transforming work of Christ that we get to express. This internal change naturally manifests externally and is intended by God to position us to change the world.

The word 'follow' in the Greek means to be 'in the same way with.' Jesus was specifically connecting this idea to being a disciple, a learner. Living a life of 'in the same way with' Jesus -- following Jesus -- is different for each person.

My family had a chance to serve the Lord through missionary work in Thailand when my hubby and I were in our young thirties. I have lived in the same town all my life and I couldn't wait to leave it. I desperately wanted to be able to say of my own life that I gave up everything to follow Jesus: my comfort, my family, my possessions, all laid down in pursuit of Him. We shortly learned that He wasn't asking us to follow Him to a land of extreme cultural differences. He was asking us to stay in our suburban Southern California hometown, become a pastor at a megachurch and live a lifestyle of being 'in the same way with,' Jesus amidst convenience and materialism.

This is obviously not everyone's journey or calling. This was ours, and I honestly mourned the loss of a dream when we said no to leaving California. I admit it -- leaving was the sexy opportunity. I felt like staying in SoCal was unadventurous and the unattractive choice.

But when Jesus says "follow me", He means to be in the same way with Him.

In my devotion, I was looking for something that would have fulfilled my desire to be "counter-cultural". While many people wouldn't be interested in a ministry so extreme as full-time third-world missions, I was interested in pursuing the opportunity to satisfy my need for adventure, new and interesting. I was willing to sacrifice something He wasn't asking for, which would have felt good for a while and then eventually turned into a disaster when I finally realized this was Christina's will and not Jesus'. The right question isn't "what are you willing to give up?" The right question is "how are you willing to live?"

Just like the man in Mark 10, you and I have been given this invitation. Have we recognized it as one and looked back into His eyes of love to offer Him our full yes?

When I reflect on the last twenty years, I can't recall a time when I woke up and said, "Today is the day I am going to meet love and be transformed." or "Today, at 4:00 pm, I will surrender and say yes fully!" Instead, I believe God hijacked random moments of my life to groom me into the person He always intended for me to be -- and He also does this with you. He intended for me to be more loving than I ever thought I could be. He intended me to look more like Him than I ever thought I could. He intended you and I live out **Ephesians 5:1-2 (NIV)** which says, "Follow God's example, therefore, as dearly loved children and walk in the way of love, just as Christ loved us and gave Himself up for us as a fragrant offering and sacrifice to God."

PASSION ALWAYS LOOKS LIKE SACRIFICE
TO PEOPLE WHO ARE NOT IN LOVE.
Kris Vallotton

AMERICAN REVIVALIST KATHRYN KULMAN started living into her destiny when she was fourteen years old in the early 1900s. After coming to know Jesus in her teen years and giving Him her full yes, she joined an evangelical team so she could share the love of Jesus that she experienced with others. Her love and gratitude for the Lord shined out of her as she would teach, minister, and share her devotion to Jesus.

Hundreds of people were healed in her meetings, and even while listening to her on the radio or television. People she prayed for would often be hit with the power of God, causing them to lose their ability to stand and fall over. Many would go into trances for hours. Kuhlman never claimed that she was the healer or powerful enough to do these things. She always pointed people to Jesus as their healer and brought an awareness of the presence of the Holy Spirit and His tenderness.

While ministering on the road, she met a man named Burroughs Waltrip who was a traveling evangelist. At the time he was married and had two small boys, yet he fell in love with Kathryn which resulted in his divorce and marriage to Kuhlman. Unfortunately, this led to the destruction of both of their public ministries.

It was necessary for Kuhlman to separate herself from the controversy connected with Borroughs "Mister" Waltrip that was bogging down her career. Judging from the rapidity with which she left Waltrip to return to her work, she instantly regretted her decision to marry him. Kuhlman faced a difficult problem. To preserve any shred of her career, she had to leave Waltrip and try to start again, but such a decision could itself destroy her.

A divorced female evangelist was not much better than a female evangelist married to a divorced man. In a masterful reinterpretation of her life, Kuhlman chose instead to present her decision to leave Waltrip as a difficult moment of submission, the yielding of a strong-willed woman to the relentless call of God on her life. Kuhlman chose to present the decision to leave her husband at the first possible moment as an act of sacrificial atonement for her defiance of God's will. She obliquely indicated throughout her career that she had realized her decision to marry Waltrip separated her from God and from her call to ministry. As she told it, the sacrifice of her marriage was necessary for her final consecration as God's instrument.[3]

After her divorce and some time to refocus, she came back to public ministry. She was a forerunner in radio and television, recording over 500 episodes in her lifetime. She spoke out about the healing power of God which resulted in unity among both the protestant and Catholic

Church. Her story is beautifully communicated in her authorized biography entitled Daughter of Destiny.[4]

Her life and ministry weren't without mistakes and sin. Neither is mine, and neither is yours. But sin isn't the focal point -- love is. She knew love at fourteen after a powerful encounter with Love Himself. As I have researched her life it looks to me as though one day, she asked herself, "Am I following Jesus still? Am I in the same way with Him today as I once was?" She wasn't questioning her salvation; she was reevaluating her devotion. When she realized that she wasn't, she course-corrected and the grace of God on her 'yes' was a catalyst for a movement and powerful healings; it impacted many people with a personal hunger for a relationship with the Holy Spirit. She finished her race well.

THE GREATEST ATTAINMENT IN THE WORLD IS FOR A LIFE TO BE SO SURRENDERED TO HIM THAT THE NAME OF GOD ALMIGHTY WILL BE GLORIFIED THROUGH THAT LIFE.
Kathryn Kuhlman

LOVE PROCEEDS AUTHORITY

THERE IS NOTHING LIKE A PROFOUND ENCOUNTER WITH GODTO INCREASE THE BURNING DESIRES OF OUR HEARTS FOR WHAT IS RIGHT AND POSSIBLE IN OUR LIFETIME.
Bill Johnson

I MENTIONED above that I noticed a similarity in the lives of all the revivalists I studied: they all had encounters with God that shaped them and defined their lives. Encounter is a simple word that denotes a face-to-face interaction. I've learned we can encounter Jesus anytime we want and that every time we do, there is an exchange. He always has good things to give us **(James 1:17)**. We can bring Him brokenness and He gives us healing. Like myself and Kathryn Kuhlman, we give Him our sin and He gives us forgiveness. We surrender our fear and He gives us peace. We give Him our attention and He gives us His love. We give Him our yes and He gives us authority. Authority from God comes in our encounters with God. Then, the power of God comes to us in the commissions He declares over us.

In Matthew 28:19, Jesus speaks over His followers what has since become known as the Great Commission. He urges those that love Him to go into the world and make disciples of all nations, baptizing them in the name of the Father, Son, and Holy Spirit. Jesus had only been with His followers for 40 days since He rose from the dead. This commission was His last epilogue. There isn't much written about how Jesus and His friends spent those last few weeks together. We have a few stories of shared meals, final fishing trips, and Jesus showing off His ability to walk through walls. He told them before His death and resurrection that it would be better for them if He left so they could be sealed with the Holy Spirit and have the presence of the living God dwelling inside of them **(John 16:7)**. Before His ascension, Jesus breathed on each of them and said, "Receive the Holy Spirit" **(John 20:22)**.

I can imagine how I would have felt if I was there standing between Peter, Andrew, and Martha. Grateful to have had 40 more days with Him, possibly betrayed at the idea that He is leaving me again. However, I'm sure somewhere deep in my heart I would have thought to myself, "Go make disciples... like, do with others what You did to me? Draw near to people and tell them about the One who touched my heart and changed my life? Then what? Show them the power of Your love? Teach others what Jesus taught me about the kingdom of God and the nature of Our Father?"

Jesus loves on the job training! He doesn't wait until we feel ready. He isn't concerned about our comfort. I can guarantee you that even after all they had seen, experienced, and done with Jesus up until that point, those eleven were all changed again after that moment of encounter and commission -- marked by their experience with Jesus and His tender love which lead to them soon turning the world upside down[5] **(Acts 17:6)**.

YEARS ago I had a vision with the Lord that came with a commission. I saw Jesus nailed to the cross before it was erected, lying on the ground. I didn't notice much of my surroundings. I was fixated on the image of Him from afar. I found myself in this vision running to Him and I threw myself on top of Him to protect Him. In my mind, I knew what I was doing was silly -- I couldn't protect Him -- but I went with what the Holy Spirit was doing. As I laid myself on top of Him, I felt He gave me a Holy Commission and whispered in my ear, "Would you be jealous for My reputation? Would you protect My real identity and dismantle every ungodly belief and lie that has been spoken about Me to My kids?" I started crying in the vision and in the natural, I said, "Yes, I will Lord with great pleasure!"

I have been in many situations where this commission has been affirmed in my life through prophetic words and dreams. I have also seen the Lord use my yes throughout my ministry experience as a common thread and great breakthrough has come from it. I am so happy I said yes! This is one of many encounters with Jesus that have changed my life and lit a fire so deep in me that even on my worst day I long for Jesus and know that I am loved and born to release His love to everyone I come into contact with. These encounters that I have had with the Lord have marked me too and have given me authority to love, to awaken the hearts of people, to be a great mom, to activate the church, to bring breakthrough into an environment, to have a strong marriage, and steward my finances with great wisdom, the list goes on.

.   .   .

AS I STARTED to grow in ministry and influence, the Lord spoke to me about sharing these personal encounters with others. Up until then, I had only shared these special moments I was having with God with a few safe people. The experiences I was having with God that I couldn't understand or the encounters that I was having that were most special I kept hidden in my heart. The more I leaned into the opportunities or invitation to an encounter, the more they would happen. I would read the Bible and start having visions. I would turn worship music on and start weeping. I would feel hot all over and be at peace for long periods of time just being in God's presence. They were tender, life-changing, all new manifestations of He and I being face-to-face.

Though I didn't share much, the people who were close to me started noticing how different I was. I was being transformed daily. What was happening inside of me was manifesting outside of me in the fruit of the spirit (Galatians 5:22) and the power of the spirit (Acts 1:8).

When the Lord asked me to share them, I mourned for two weeks the loss of my "secret" history with the Lord!

I wasn't terrified that people were going to abandon me or call me a heretic. I had been heart connected to the Lord for years and the fear of man was burned off of me in an encounter I will tell you about later. I was mourning because it was so special, private, and intimate. I didn't want those moments to be put on display or for people to say it wasn't real or they didn't matter. But then it hit me: no matter what people said about my encounters -- the fruit of being with Jesus, being transformed by Him -- was evident in my life. God even had a friend speak over me the same phrase, "Christina, the fruit from your life speaks for itself," and all my doubts were silenced.

It was an unexpected emotional rollercoaster as I dealt with the reality that my moments with Him weren't just about the two of us anymore; they were about releasing faith for what's possible in a relationship with Jesus. I was growing, learning, and taking new risks, and the Lord was wanting to use me and my time with Him to encourage other people to be with Him as well. Just like those I enjoyed reading about in biographies and in church history books!

I've thought about it a lot as I've navigated my own journey of surrender as a follower of Jesus. I've been fulfilled, hidden, nameless, and on a covert mission. I wonder if the people I've read about throughout the years felt the same way? These heroes of mine: revivalist, presidents, missionaries, and leaders never set out to impress me or tell me their story, but I learned more about who God is and isn't from their experiences and lives.

I gained faith every time I heard a testimony or researched how God changed a person's life **(Romans 10:17)**. I needed to trust Him to do that with my life; the breakthrough and healing I had been a part of, the supernatural events that were experienced on the pages of my story, needed to be read by others as well. He wanted to use me to bring an awakening to the hearts of His people and put His goodness on display!

"Completely shocked by Jesus' answer, he turned and walked away very sad, for he was extremely rich. **Mark 10:21 (TPT)** Remember, it wasn't that he didn't know how to love, it's that he didn't know how to love the right thing. I didn't want to make the same mistake. I didn't want to love my history with Him more than my future with Him. I didn't want to hoard something He was asking me to give away. He was giving me an opportunity to invest what He had given me into the soil of His people's hearts.

I had to take a risk and I am so glad that I did. I've seen it multiply, I've seen more miracles and love poured out than I could have imagined. I've seen more breakthroughs and hope released than I would have if I remained silent. I never knew His love would lead me to burn and set other people on fire as well. My vision for my life was so much smaller than He had for me.

I'm glad I learned to love the right thing. I'm glad to call myself His disciple and receive His commission. Just as it is impossible to encounter Jesus and not be changed, it is impossible to burn for Him and not have something happen. I am honored to carry His flame of love -- to have encountered a personal revival in my soul that has become a lifestyle of revival! Anyone who has encountered the love of God is meant to be a revivalist.

THE BEST OF ALL, GOD IS WITH US.
John Wesley

4

LIVING WITH OR LIVING WITHOUT

LIVE READY.
IF YOU HAVE TO GET READY
WHEN OPPORTUNITY COMES YOUR
WAY, YOU ARE TOO LATE.
Smith Wigglesworth

IT'S time to share one of the most significant encounters that marked me forever with you, and I do so gladly -- not for personal boasting but as I have said, to create faith for the possibility and to put the realness, closeness, and heart of our God on display!

It was a regular weekday morning. I wasn't in a hurry, but I also wasn't planning on getting wrecked by God that day.

In fact, I was tired. I had been running hard in life, family, relationship, and service -- all things ministry (in my opinion)! All good and necessary things, but true to form, I had neglected to build some margin in my life and I was feeling the effects of the lack of rest. My M.O. is very fast-paced. I take on new projects in a sprint and I tend to run until they're truly done. Sometimes it feels like a gift, and sometimes it feels like a curse!

I was waking up and immediately encountered the Lord's presence.[6] I was face-to-face with Him in my imagination. He didn't walk into the room physically, I didn't see a vision externally, but in my spirit, in my mind, I knew I was in His presence.

I learned years ago that God gave us our imaginations to connect with Him. **1 John 5:20 (NASB)** says, "...God has given us an understanding that we may know Him." The word for understanding can also be translated as "imagination". I connect with the Lord best this way. It wasn't always a part of my history with Him (we will dive into more about this later) but as I grew in my devotion and my hunger to connect to His voice and heart, I gave Him permission to meet me in this way. It changed my relationship with Him forever.[7]

I am convinced this wasn't just speculation or the effects of being a high-level daydreamer! When I encounter the Lord like this, I see things I am not creative enough to imagine. I learn things about His character that I am not smart enough to understand through study - He invites me to experience Him instead. Upon awakening and connecting to His invitation to join Him that morning, I saw a door open and Jesus was standing in front of a mirror. He was dressed in a fine tuxedo. He looked handsome and I recognized the Holy Spirit who was swirling around Him. I instantly knew He was getting ready to wed His bride.[8]

I came up to Him and ran my fingers through his hair, fixing it for Him. I kissed Him on His cheek. Then I started dusting off His lapel and straightening His bow tie. Understanding that He was about to walk down the aisle and be joined with His bride, I looked into His eyes and blessed Him to receive the love of His life like never before. It was similar to something a parent would say to their loved one on the day of their wedding!

I remember saying to Jesus, "I bless You to receive entirely what Your heart has been longing for in humanity since the beginning of time. I bless You to have great intimacy with Your new bride. That the time you spend together would be fun, fabulous, and fulfilling. I know you have been waiting for this day for such a long time! I bless you to live into the delight and excitement of marrying your bride!" I was proud of Him like a parent would be. I noticed as I looked at His demeanor He was almost bursting out at the seams. He was so very happy and so excited for this day.

I spent some time in this vision admiring how He looked. The look in His eyes was especially fascinating to me. He was so confident and full of love. Funnily enough -- yes, I know this doesn't make perfect sense, just keep reading -- He even had butterflies in His stomach. He was nervous like any man would be in this situation. We hugged and He left; He walked out of the room, and I watched as Father God came and hugged Him. They soon walked down the aisle both filled with great pride and love for each other. Then I recognized the Holy Spirit in the room with me. He was next to walk down the aisle. I stayed in the room and watched as He went out to the ceremony to be with His family.

That was it.

I didn't ask any questions. I didn't freak out, tell all my friends or stay in bed waiting for an angel to appear. I just got up brushed my teeth like any normal person would and started my day. For the next few days, I thought often about the look on Jesus' face and what I had just been given the privilege to observe.

A few days later I was out of town visiting a church in Los Angeles, California. The worship experience was utter bliss! The sound wasn't perfect, there were no lights flashing, no fog machine running, no world-class production team in the back. It was pretty bare bones. I was caught up hearing everyone around singing in beautiful pure worship. We were all seeking God's face not His hand. It was different. There was honor and adoration going up to the throne of God and while I was both assessing the atmosphere and pouring out my own worship to the Lord, I heard Jesus say, "This is what you blessed me to receive."

I paused. I didn't understand what He meant at first until the Lord reminded me of my encounter a few days earlier. I was in that moment of worship experiencing what my heart had days earlier and I realized I was seeing what I prayed for: Jesus experiencing the joy of His wedding to His bride and being loved by her. This was the second part of that vision.

I was shaking and crying, and I started sweating -- a manifestation that happens often when His power and Spirit are on me. Instantly, my energy was being restored to my heart and body. The fatigue, the extreme tiredness and exhaustion, all burnout was being burned off of me! I sat down in my seat. I couldn't stand to worship anymore. I was shaking and sweating and crying. I saw again in my imagination all the things that my heart longs for in words floating around my head. Words like justice, truth, encounters, love, His name glorified, all came together in the moment of bliss. I felt that He was not only restoring my energy but re-engaging me with His vision for my life.

It became a holy moment again of exchange and surrender. I repented from pulling my heart away from His people and His bride. I told Him I was sorry for getting to a place where I was so tired. When I am tired, I entertain thoughts of quitting and criticism. I repented for both those things and told Him that I wasn't ever going to quit seeing His bride made ready for Him! I would continue to work toward that end -- her preparation for the ceremony!! There was a puddle of tears below me. I told Him, "I love that You know me... that I am known by You." And He responded, "I am so happy to be known BY YOU!" and I lost it even more.

There were more tears, more shaking, more sweating than if I had run a marathon. I don't know why those things happen to me when I see Him face-to-face. It also doesn't happen that way each time. This was a profound moment in my life that has been the catalyst for great resolve and grit as I've served Him throughout the years, but also it has given me a great love for those that I get to serve. The image of Jesus in His tuxedo and His bride awaiting her groom is so burned into my heart and soul that rarely a day goes by that I don't think about it. Though massively unexplainable and slightly irrational it's the motivation I keep as I engage my challenge of how far love will take me.

The apostle John had a similar encounter with Jesus when he was on the island of Patmos. The revelation of Jesus to John in Chapter 4 of the book of Revelation reads like this:

> After this I looked, and there before me was a door standing open in heaven. And the voice I had first heard speaking to me like a trumpet said, "Come up here, and I will show you what must take place after this." At once I was in the Spirit, and there before me was a throne in heaven with someone sitting on it. And the one who sat there had the appearance of jasper and ruby. A rainbow that shone like an emerald encircled the throne. Surrounding the throne were twenty-four other thrones and seated on them were twenty-four elders. They were dressed in white and had crowns of gold on their heads. From the throne came flashes of lightning, rumblings and peals of thunder. In front of the throne, seven lamps were blazing. These are the seven spirits of God. Also, in front of the throne there was what looked like a sea of glass, clear as crystal.
>
> In the center, around the throne, were four living creatures, and they were covered with eyes, in front and in back. The first living creature was like a lion, the second was like an ox, the third had a face like a man, the fourth was like a flying eagle. Each of the four living creatures had six wings and was covered with eyes all around, even under its wings. Day and night they never stop saying:

"'Holy, holy, holy
is the Lord God Almighty,
who was, and is, and is to come."
Revelation 4:1-9

I don't understand all of John's vision, and maybe you don't understand all of mine. I imagine that the awe and wonder, even the majesty of the things understood and things beyond comprehension left him feeling overwhelmed and honored as a participant. He also realized he was being commissioned to be a messenger of the revelation of Jesus Christ. He was given this revelation to give away as a messenger to the church.

Throughout the Bible the encounters God had with His people are crazy! Let's call a spade a spade! Even since Bible days, revivalists that have gone before us have had some hard-to-believe encounters with the Lord! I used to try to analyze and interpret them. I also tried to find validity in scripture for every wild encounter I had or heard about. Some I could prove in scripture, and some I couldn't. Then I read,

Psalms 115:3 (NIV) which says, "Our God is in heaven; He does what pleases Him."

So, I stopped questioning and chose to be mystified by Jesus instead. The fruit will always represent the fruit tree! Built into each encounter we have with the Lord is healing, breakthrough, and revelation. Every time Jesus shows up, He shows off. It is also in the encounter that Jesus gives His kids His authority and then a commission to go with it!

Before the encounter I mentioned above I didn't know the outflow of my heart was to see the heart needs of Jesus met in such a way that my life would be forever marked by loving His bride and kids! It has become my reason for getting out of bed in the morning, the reason I take risks, pursue maturity, and desire to grow. The reason is, as my husband says, I can't just smoke a cigar without talking about changing the world.

One of the craziest things about the Lord is that He probably wanted me to be possessed by this promise when I received that prophetic word in my teenage years about faith and healing. At that time I was intrigued but not interested, yet the Lord never changed His mind about my destiny or His heart for me **(Romans 11:29)**.

I didn't steward the invitation when I was younger. I had a series of opportunities as the years went on to choose differently. It wasn't until I chose to surrender fully to the plans of the Lord for my life that I actually grabbed onto the destiny that He had been saving for me. My agreement with it again came with an exchange. I surrendered my pride, my secrets, my intent, and He gave me a love that's better than I ever experienced and a destiny that freaks me out!

I DON'T GO TO RELIGION TO MAKE ME HAPPY. I ALWAYS KNEW A BOTTLE OF PORT WOULD DO THAT. IF YOU WANT A RELIGION TO MAKE YOU FEEL REALLY COMFORTABLE, I CERTAINLY DON'T RECOMMEND CHRISTIANITY.
C.S. Lewis

THE COST OF SURRENDER

GOD, I WILL MAKE WAR WITH EVERYTHING THAT SEEKS TO USURP THE INWARD FLAME OF DEVOTION IN MY LIFE.
Lou Engle

MARK RECOUNTS a story of love and surrender.

Mark writes that Jesus was in Bethany, chilling at the table in the home of a friend when a familiar woman came in with a jar of very expensive perfume:

> She broke the jar and poured the perfume on His head. Some of those present were saying indignantly to one another, "Why this waste of perfume? It could have been sold for more than a year's wages and the money given to the poor." And they rebuked her harshly. "Leave her alone," said Jesus. "Why are you bothering her?

She has done a beautiful thing to Me. The poor you will always have with you, and you can help them any time you want. But you will not always have Me. She did what she could. She poured perfume on My body beforehand to prepare for My burial. Truly I tell you, wherever the gospel is preached throughout the world, what she has done will also be told, in memory of her." **Mark 14:1-9 (TPT)**

Great teachers have shared about this passage of scripture, and Jesus' words are true -- her legacy of love lived on far beyond her lifespan.

However, if we read these words as a story and never acknowledged the invitation, we will have missed the significance. This woman barged into an environment where she wasn't wanted. She didn't have the right to attend. Amidst men who didn't approve of her and could have stoned her for her presence, she approached Jesus, the only man who ever treated her with kindness. She worshipped Him with such extravagance that she wasted her livelihood, her retirement plan, her plan A and probably B on Him. She gave a gift that cost her everything and it became the sweetest worship to the Lord. It ministered to Him personally.

I once heard a teacher suggest that the amount of perfume was so extravagant that not only did she physically prepare Jesus for His burial which was fast approaching, but it was likely that as He was being scourged and crucified the fragrance would have seeped from His wounds. The aroma could have been recognized and smelt in the air. During a time of intense physical pain and surrender for Jesus, He was able to gain strength through the worship and adoration by the bride He was suffering for.

Can you imagine the effects of her gift to Jesus when He needed it most? The great comfort it brought to Him? We are the joy set before Him as He endured the suffering of His death. **(Hebrews 12:2)** The thought of you, the image of you in His mind is what He focused on so He could give Himself as a gift to us! Anything I have to give Him is out of my love for Him, just like He gave Himself out of His love for us. What a thought!

We see in this woman's example that she gave it all to her King. Not out of duty or obligation -- purely out of love. Not out of wanting a platform, ministry, or acknowledgment from man. On the contrary, in the face of great danger her surrender was so genuine it blinded her to the risk that she took in the room. Or maybe she wasn't blind to it, maybe she was fully aware and simply didn't care. She had this one chance to surrender, to give it all away as her offering, her gift to the One who had given her everything she really needed.

It reminds me of King David. We read about his surrender and heart to give extravagantly in **1 Chronicles**:

> Then the angel of the Lord ordered Gad to tell David to go up and build an altar to the Lord on the threshing floor of Araunah the Jebusite. So David went up in obedience to the word that Gad had spoken in the name of the Lord.

> While Araunah was threshing wheat, he turned and saw the angel; his four sons who were with him hid themselves. Then David approached, and when Araunah looked and saw him, he left the threshing floor and bowed down before David with his face to the ground.

> David said to him, "Let me have the site of your threshing floor so I can build an altar to the Lord, that the plague on the people may be stopped. Sell it to me at the full price."

> Araunah said to David, "Take it! Let my lord the king do whatever pleases him. Look, I will give the oxen for the burnt offerings, the threshing sledges for the wood, and the wheat for the grain offering. I will give all this." But King David replied to Araunah, "No, I insist on paying the full price. I will not take for the Lord what is yours, or sacrifice a burnt offering that costs me nothing."

1 Chronicles 21:18-24 (NIV)

David recognized he needed to give an offering to the Lord that cost something, even when he could get away with offering nothing. King David replied to a generous offer, "No, I insist on paying the full price. I will not take from the Lord what is yours, or sacrifice a burnt offering that costs me nothing" (vs 24). I will not offer something that costs me nothing. Here we have the king of Israel, who understood what it meant to be a priest to the Lord, to be a minister to God. David knew that his offering -- his gift -- should cost him something.

There is an exchange that happens in surrender. I suggest that exchange happens the moment we say 'yes' and are willing to risk something we treasure for the sake of love. Like the rich young ruler, the woman at Bethany, and King David with the field -- they had to be willing to risk something important to them as an expression of their love for their King. Could this be what happens as we worship? Could this be the invitation available for every human being, or is it limited to these three? Could it be that destinies, inheritances, miracles, and transformation hang off the floors of heaven, intended for our reach, as we decide whether or not we are going to give extravagantly and choose to be all in?

IN OUR ABANDONMENT, WE GIVE OURSELVES OVER TO GOD
JUST AS GOD GAVE HIMSELF FOR US, WITHOUT ANY
CALCULATIONS. THE CONSEQUENCES OF ABANDONMENT
NEVER ENTER INTO OUR OUTLOOK
BECAUSE OUR LIFE IS TAKEN UP IN HIM.
Oswald Chambers

YOU CAN HAVE IT ALL GOD

EVERYTHING IF GIVEN TO GOD CAN
BECOME YOUR GATEWAY TO JOY
Elizabeth Elliot

I've had multiple moments of surrendering to the Lord. When I realized I needed salvation at five years old; every year at high school summer camp when it just felt good to get saved again; when I decided to run from my own stubbornness and independence and reclaim my relationship with God as my Lord. I think surrender comes in layers as we build trust with God and grow in a desire to trust Him.

One of the most profound moments of surrender happened when I decided to give up the one thing I told the Lord I would never give up. It wasn't an ongoing sin; it wasn't a destructive habit. It was a secret that I swore I would die keeping. I kept this secret for over ten years. Sometimes intentionally I found myself working hard to keep it. Some weeks went by and I didn't even think about it. I would often find myself singing in worship,

"You can have it all God," (but I would whisper in my heart, "except for this")...

"Every part of my world," (and follow it with, "but this one area we have a deal righhhhht")...

"Take this life and breath on this heart that is 95% yours."

At the time I had a great family, and I was experiencing being used by the Lord to see people break out of sin, strongholds, and fear. I was teaching, leading ministries, and very fulfilled, but as time went on, I would feel burdened with the fear of being exposed. I told the Lord in a failed attempt to negotiate, "We have a great thing going on -- no need to share this or rock the boat. You can keep using me like this and I will give you everything I am... except this one thing and I will not ask for any more from You. A deal is a deal."

I was living a better, more satisfied life than I ever imagined. He didn't have to trust me with any more responsibility as long as I could keep my secret. I don't ever remember Him agreeing with the deal but I definitely held up my end... until I just couldn't anymore.

The truth is, you're only as free as the secrets you keep.

I've helped so many people get free, but when it was time to deal with my heart and my process, I forgot the same grace that I taught over and over again could be personally appropriated. Instead, I decided to allow my mind to be stuck in tormenting thoughts that discredited the fullness of my value, identity, and purpose. It's easy to retreat when your sins are being brought to light. It's easy in that place to reduce your calling to what you think you deserve in your weakest moments. This is a great lie from hell! I agreed with it for ten years. I made fear my home and some days it didn't cost me, but as the years went on it became a burden too heavy to bear.

So I faced my fear, surrendered my deal to the Lord, and immediately cleaned up my mess with those my secret affected. I remember feeling exhausted. As though had I just come out of a ten-year battle. I didn't feel warm and fuzzy inside. You know how your mom tries to tell you when you're young and you get caught in a lie, "Just tell the truth and you will feel better." That wasn't true. I didn't feel better. I felt tired and vulnerable.

The next day I spent time with the Lord, and I asked Him why I didn't really feel any different. This act of surrender was a big deal and I thought it would feel like a big deal. I mean, I protected this thing for years! I spent so much energy and time in hiding. Surely something must be different after yielding to the Lord. I asked for forgiveness again, thinking maybe I didn't do it right the first time. Obviously, that had nothing to do with it, so I asked the Lord, "What am I missing in this situation?"

The Holy Spirit told me I had made an agreement with shame to keep it as my punisher for the ten-year indiscretion. Even though I was forgiven for keeping the secret, I still kept shame so I could feel repentant. I was forgiven but not clean. His intention is to do both, and He tells us this in **1 John 1:9 (NLT)**, But if we confess our sins to Him, He is faithful and just to forgive us our sins and to cleanse us from all wickedness.

As I laid out on my bed weeping, I invited the Lord to clean me and take away all the shame. I saw the Holy Spirit in my imagination, and His eyes were burning through me. There are no secrets between Him and I. He saw right through me and did not look disappointed, disgusted, or ashamed of me. There was only love. So much love.

I knew I could keep shame as my punisher and simply be forgiven or I could hand it over to Him and make an exchange in my surrender. I chose the latter, so I asked the Lord, "As I give you my shame, my shame and my need for a punisher, what do you want to give me in exchange?" The Holy Spirit told me to stand in front of a mirror, look at myself, and yell out, "I'm unashamed and worthy of love." I did this so many times -- 30 or 40 -- until it became a revelation to my spirit and my mind. This encounter brought me into a commission and a new way of experiencing life, not limited to the absence of shame but filled with the power to live unashamed, whole, and clean.

A white flag is a well-known symbol of surrender. This symbol dates back to centuries of war. But the white flag is often only the first step toward a treaty. Sometimes the surrender is marked by the laying down of weapons, a new loyalty to the winning country, a kiss placed on the commanding officer's hand. It normally is followed by an exchange. A written document called a peace treaty would be drafted declaring alliance and the new terms of the covenant with each other.

The cost of the surrender may be a nation's pride, their independence, a way of life, the loss of control. I wonder if these are the best "weapons" we can surrender at the Lord's feet. There is a cost to surrender. We avoid it for many reasons, yet it brings the peace we long for. It can happen in a radical moment, a gradual process, or over our lifetime. We were meant to be at peace with God through Jesus **(Romans 5:1)**, and that peace is a better way to live than holding on to our "weapons" and our "deals".

Looking back, I realize that there is a marked difference between what I thought was a full life with God (while still holding on to my secret) and my life with Him now. I have discovered from personal experience that as Christians, we tend to think, "I wonder how much I can get away with and still be effective in ministry or still move in signs and wonders?" What a shame that thought crosses our minds. It is not about how far we can go and still have power. It should be that all power and ability of the Holy Spirit in our lives does nothing for us unless we are in connection with the vine **(John 10)**.

The Amplified Bible describes that as Jesus was dying on the cross, He asked God, "Why have you forsaken me, deserted me, leaving me helpless and abandoned."[9]

Can you imagine it -- the cost of surrender at this moment and Jesus being helpless? I've heard countless sermons about the finished work of the cross and His last words. I've never thought about Jesus being helpless. At this moment, Jesus was still God. His deity had not been taken away. His supernatural abilities still remained. The Holy Spirit showed me that what rendered Him helpless wasn't a lack of power or ability. It was the lack of intimacy with His Father in the moment.

True surrender results in a peace treaty that puts the rightful king on the throne of our hearts. It's our opportunity to make an alliance with the King of Kings so we can live under the intention and order of His Kingdom which is built on love. It's in this place of surrender and encounter we receive His commissioning and purposes for our lives which includes His passions, will, and value system. We become living flames of love sent out from His heart to represent Him and His kingdom to the world around us. This fire is ours to keep lit and where revival becomes a lifestyle.

MATURE PEOPLE HAVE A PASSION FOR THE PRESENCE OF GOD, WHICH IS GREATER THAN THEIR ZEAL FOR MINISTRY. PEOPLE WHO ARE WONDERFULLY ANOINTED IN MINISTRY BUT VERY AVERAGE IN INTIMACY ARE NOT MATURE.
Graham Cooke

5

BORN TO BURN

WHAT WE NEED IS A FRESH VISION OF THE CROSS. AND MAY THAT MIGHTY, ALL EMBRACING LOVE OF HIS BE NO LONGER A FITFUL, WAVERING INFLUENCE IN OUR LIVES, BUT THE RULING PASSION OF OUR SOULS.
Evan Roberts

THE SOLUTION to every moral failure, every broken family, every power-hungry nation, every corrupt government, is in the fire of God on the Earth burning in the hearts of His sons and daughters. The solution to every area of our lives is to burn. It's one way we honor Jesus' life, death, and resurrection in our life. It's what we were born for.

REVELATION IS the place where the fire of God can be invited. Revelation and information are not the same. Information can be described simply as facts learned. Revelation happens when facts are experienced. Consider the difference between reading about how to ride a horse, and actually climbing up into a saddle. You can read for days and learn lots of information but once you get on the horse, feel the powerful animal beneath you and notice the chaffing in your calves and pain from the saddle -- that, my friend, is revelation. Some things you simply cannot learn through information.

PETER IS MY FAVORITE DISCIPLE. I'm not uncommon in my preference -- we all love Peter because we all identify with him! We know what it feels like to have a mountain top experience one moment and get put in our place the next! Peter had many profound encounters with Jesus that gave him the revelation about the Lordship of Jesus which have been used to shape our relationship and understanding of Him as well.

Take **Matthew 16** for example. Jesus is hanging out with His followers, men and women who had given up everything to become His apprentices, He turns to them and asks, "Who are people saying I am?" They responded with a list of the most current commentary until Jesus changes the subject without changing His language. He asks, "Who do you say that I am?" And Peter answered, "You are the Messiah, the Son of the living God." Jesus replied, "Blessed are you, Simon son of Jonah, for this was not revealed to you by flesh and blood, but by My Father in heaven **Matthew 16:16-17 (NIV)**.

Jesus asked a very interesting question. He wasn't needing to know for Himself -- He wasn't experiencing an identity crisis or trying to take a poll on His popularity. He was extending an invitation into revelation. Jesus asked His friends, "Who am I to you?" This question is so powerful! It becomes the foundation we build our lives on **(Matthew 7:24)**.

We can invite the fire of God to come and burn in us by pursuing more revelation of God. Or let me say it this way: the altar of revelation is where you invite the fire of God to come and burn. The fire of God cleanses us, gives us passion, creates zeal, and empowers us to evangelize and heal. It purifies us, changes us, and makes us more like Him. It was meant for us to experience (revelation not information). It results in devotion and consecration. It connects us to Him and His ways. Interestingly, 'fire' in the Greek is the same word for 'purge' or 'clean.'

The Bible talks about the fire of God often. There are references to Him in fire, having eyes of fire, and being an all-consuming fire. He sends fire from heaven as a sign, goes into a fire with His boys, and also promises that when we are in the fire we will not be burned. Every reference is powerful and a mystery.

We were made to live in passion, in love, and on fire. This passion -- this fire -- that most people experience when they are first saved through the revelation of Jesus is supposed to be with us always, just like His spirit is always with us (Ephesians 1:13). It is never intended to be a small flame on its way to dying out, but a roaring fire.

BILL JOHNSON SAID it like this:

> Being lukewarm in our relationship with Jesus is not a season, it's a devil. It is simply not necessary to be lukewarm. We have challenges in our lives, trials, emotional times but none of that ever has to translate to complacency in our devotion to Jesus. Never is complacency an answer. Never have I been reduced to a routine in Jesus.

I want to be able to say the same thing, and I want you to as well! Call to mind someone you know who lives out this burning passion for the Lord. Picture them in your imagination and what it is about their life, how they live, that causes you to think of them as a fiery one? I hope you have many people that come to your mind. And now add another -- yourself -- to the image. See yourself as a single living flame joining together with the others to form a raging fire of zeal for the Lord. I believe it is possible and the will of God, that we burn with passion and devotion for Jesus Christ all our days.

FATHER, MAKE OF ME A CRISIS MAN. BRING THOSE I CONTACT TO DECISION. LET ME NOT BE A MILEPOST ON A SINGLE ROAD; MAKE ME A FORK, THAT MEN MUST TURN ONE WAY OR ANOTHER ON FACING CHRIST IN ME.
Jim Elliot

WHO OWNS IT?

ACTION SPRINGS NOT FROM THOUGHT,
BUT FROM A READINESS FOR RESPONSIBILITY.
Dietrich Bonhoeffer

Let's consider the Old Testament model of the priests and their sacrifices as we learn practically what this looks like to burn with a passion all the days of our lives:

"Then the Lord said to Moses, "Give Aaron and his sons the following instructions regarding the burnt offering. The burnt offering must be left on top of the altar until the next morning, and the fire on the altar must be kept burning all night. In the morning, after the priest on duty has put on his official linen clothing and linen undergarments, he must clean out the ashes of the burnt offering and put them beside the altar. Then he must take off these garments, change back into his regular clothes, and carry the ashes outside the camp to a place that is ceremonially clean. Meanwhile, the fire on the altar must be kept burning; it must never go out. Each morning the priest will add fresh wood to the fire and arrange the burnt offering on it. he will then burn the fat of the peace offerings on it. Remember, the fire must be kept burning on the altar at all times. It must never go out." **Leviticus 6:8-13 (NLT)**

What do you notice is the main point of the above text in regard to the role of the priest? Why would the Lord make it a requirement for the priests to keep the fire burning on the altar?

A burnt offering is an Old Testament act of worship, a sacrifice, or an offering. In this passage we see the priest's role was very specific: they were to keep the fire on the altar burning at all times. Aaron served as the first High Priest. All of his male descendants were chosen by God to be priests forever; it was an eternal covenant, not just a commandment or cultural rule.

When Jesus came and brought His kids into the new covenant **(Hebrews 8:8-12)**, we were all set apart as priests. As Peter tells us in **1 Peter 2:9 (NIV)**, "But you are a chosen people, a royal priesthood, a holy nation, God's special possession, that you may declare the praises of Him who called you out of darkness into his wonderful light." The job description of the Old Testament priest is not a role synonymous with our modern-day lead pastor. Our pastors are priests of the Lord alongside everyone who calls themselves a follower of Jesus. This includes you and me, which then puts responsibility for our devotion into our hands. It is ours to own. It is not the church's job, my pastor's job, or my friend's job to light my fire! I am a priest of the Lord and my fire is my responsibility. John Wesley was once asked, "What is your secret? Why do so many people come to hear you preach?" Wesley answered, "I get alone with God in prayer. He sets me on fire. Then people come out to watch me burn."

Let's take it one step further. If we look back to the fellowship of the early Church before it was institutionalized, we see men and women gathered together in homes acting as ministers and priests of the Lord:

> They devoted themselves to the apostles' teaching and to fellowship, to the breaking of bread and to prayer. Everyone was filled with awe at the many wonders and signs performed by the apostles. All the believers were together and had everything in common. They sold property and possessions to give to anyone who had need. Every day

they continued to meet together in the temple courts. They broke bread in their homes and ate together with glad and sincere hearts, praising God and enjoying the favor of all the people. And the Lord added to their number daily those who were being saved. **Acts 2:42-47 (NIV)**

As they met everyone had a role. As an active part of living out their devotion to the Lord, they were expected to share an impromptu message of what Jesus was saying to them, confess their sins to one another, pray for healing and salvation, lead their friends in communion, and give to those in need. In essence, they were individually maintaining their own intimacy with the Lord in such a way that when they gathered it was many flames igniting as one raging fire. This, my friends, is Christian living! Everyone attending to fire on the altar of the hearts as a daily practice and responsibility. It wasn't until Constantine legalized Christianity and gatherings moved from houses of Acts to large buildings which shifted the focus from the responsibility of every priest of the Lord to the most effective speaker who could captivate the largest crowd.

As Rutz says, "When we switched from living rooms to church buildings and professionally staffed the local church, we lost all momentum. The local church became weak and cold."[10]

This is not a theological conversation about Ekklesia. That will be another book! I am also not hating on pastors and the buildings we gather in. What I am saying is that throughout church history, many generations of Christians have forgotten who owns the responsibility of being in love. We recognize how to fall in love. We don't take ownership of the relationship that it takes to remain in love and maintain our fire. I love pastors; I am one. But it is not my role to collect firewood and add it to your altar. It is not my role to watch over your flame while you go to work. Everyone owns their own fire.

It's hard to stand in the gaze of one whose eyes are like fire and not burn. The simple reality is that God built personal responsibility into our relationship with Him. We own it! It is proportionate to any relationship we have. We cannot force anyone to love us, and we cannot control anyone else's process. We cannot expect to stay married if we do not engage with our spouses. It's that simple. We harvest what we put time into cultivating. Similarly, we can't talk, debate, or force anyone to burn with affection for the Lord. We can't persuade anybody into finishing well or being a good Christian. All we can do is burn and invite others to come along.

As Paul's life is a framework for me knowing I can finish my race well (**2 Timothy 4:7**), our lives can become the framework to spark a hunger in others as we release the possibilities of what our relationship with the Lord and revival should look like to the world around us. It comes from personal revelation and responsibility. Can you hear the questions of our King asking the same thing to all of us, "Who am I to you?"

TO ATTEND TO HIM (GOD) IN MINISTRY IS THE GREATEST PRIVILEGE THAT WE HAVE AS HUMAN BEINGS AND IT IS OFFERED TO EVERY ONE OF US. THROUGH JESUS' DEATH WE ARE ABLE TO COME FACE TO FACE BEFORE THE LORD AND LIFT UP OUR OFFERINGS OF THANKSGIVING AND PRAISE FOR WHO HE IS.
Bill Johnson

THE BAPTISM OF FIRE

GOD'S PURPOSE FOR MY LIFE WAS THAT I HAVE A PASSION FOR GOD'S GLORY AND THAT I HAVE A PASSION FOR MY JOY IN THAT GLORY, AND THAT THESE TWO ARE ONE PASSION.

Jonathan Edwards

JOHN THE BAPTIST, spoke out a powerful prophetic declaration about Jesus, "But John made it clear by telling them, "There is One coming who is mightier than I. He is supreme. In fact, I'm not worthy of even being His slave. I can only baptize you in this river, but He will baptize you into the Spirit of holiness and into His raging fire. **Luke 3:16 (TPT)** Brian Simmons writes in the footnotes of the Passion Translation for this verse:

> The Aramaic text reads 'He will baptize you into the Spirit of the Holy One and in light.' A baptism of light or fire would cleanse and change a life, giving new power to live for God and deal with every issue that hinders love and passion from burning in our hearts. It is the baptism of the Holy Spirit that is needed today.

This is a great visual of a small portion of what the fire of God does. The fire of God provides power to live for God and deal with every issue that hinders love and passion for the kingdom of God. Some people refer to this as the "baptism of fire." Some denominations teach on this, some churches pray it over their people or have fire tunnels to invite it. This is also a military term used to communicate heavy fire in combat or an initial experience that is a severe ordeal. It reminds me of when our three kids all had the stomach flu at the same time. We went from kid to kid all night with no sleep holding trash cans, changing sheets, feeding them Pedialyte only to catch it as it came back up. Baptism of fire right there.

The baptism of fire from the Lord (while similarly intense) is a much better experience. I have encountered this a few times and can confirm that His fire cleanses and gives new power! Remember, we receive authority in the encounter and power in the commission.

I WAS READING a book one afternoon about a current revivalist and missionary named Heidi Baker. My three kids were in the backyard playing together (first miracle) and I heard the whisper of the Lord ask,

"Do you want to hang out?" I do want to pause to bring a deeper understanding to what I am saying when I say I "heard" God's whisper. When we externally hear sounds the sound waves enter our outer ear and travel through our ear canal, which leads to our eardrum. That is not what I am describing. I've never heard from God this way as some people describe the audible voice of God. One day I know I will! But until then, I have learned to discern the voice of God internally.

This kind of hearing happens in my mind through my thoughts -- some people describe this way of hearing as an "impression".[11] This is a very common way people recognize the voice of the Lord and it is tricky to identify for many of us since it often sounds like our own voice. If it takes you a while to realize it is Him -- He doesn't mind! He is very patient with us and actually enjoys our process.

Jesus brought me on a journey a few years ago to recognize this as a way He speaks to me. In the same way that my imagination is a tool that I can use to encounter Him, I have discovered that my thoughts often are from Him. He brought me through a beautiful journey (still ongoing) of risk, trust, and testing my ability to identify His Spirit and voice through impressions.

This day I was still in the middle of my learning journey, so I paused as I second-guessed what I was hearing in my thoughts as from the Spirit of God. In the learning, He taught me to trust His ability to speak to me more than Satan's ability to deceive me. So I responded, I put my book down and leaned in. I told Him, "Yes I do want to hang out with You! And I have a question! What happens when I worship?" Worship was not on my mind as I was reading but for whatever reason Jesus is awesome and wanted to heal me of something in this moment.

Immediately, I pictured Father God's face. He was clear and regal, but I could barely look into his eyes. Suddenly my physical body started shaking and I broke out into a weeping cry. I could barely even swallow. I felt so heavy. I kept trying to look back and lock in a gaze with His eyes, but for some reason, I couldn't do it. Father God spoke and He said to me, "Don't turn away from Me. I never turn away from you."

I lifted my hands and remained engaged in my vision even though I was physically shaking and crying and kept moving my eyes away. It was as if His eyes of fire were so purifying and so loving that things were melting and burning off me. Within a few minutes, I could stay face-to-face fixed on his eyes. At first, I thought He was melting off my sin, but then I realized it wasn't sin -- it was rejection.

I immediately remembered a time years earlier when I was studying music in college. I would spend ten hours a week practicing and preparing songs to sing in front of my voice teacher. More hours learning how to pronounce and sing words in German, Latin, Italian, and French. Even more hours listening to opera singers I wanted to sound like. I gave myself entirely to this passion. One day I went into my weekly voice lesson and sang the aria I had spent so long practicing. My voice teacher said that in the entire song, two sounds were lovely.

I didn't think much of it at the time. I mean, don't get me wrong it hurt! It was frustrating and painful but the heavy critique, the comparison, the demand for perfectionism were all a part of the process. This was what the Lord wanted to heal in my vision. This was why He came with a baptism of fire. As Brian Simmons said, "To burn away every issue that hinders love and passion."

I learned the fear of man through my vocal coach. I brought my best and it wasn't good enough. I was criticized and it was painful in ways I didn't even realize at the time. My gift was rejected, and in that room, I learned my best wasn't good enough. I started to believe the lie that I wasn't good enough. Inadequacy, rejection, and fear of man had taken up residence in my life and became a part of my operating system. Sometimes it was overt and affected my relationships, influence, environments, and emotional safety; sometimes it was subtle and only defeated me. In this moment of encounter, when the Lord of Hosts was staring at me with His eyes of fire, these places of rejection and woundedness were now withering from my life. They were being removed and I was experiencing the way the Lord was healing me through His touch -- and it caused me to shake and weep.

I can't explain fully how I knew what He was doing. It happened in natural time very quickly, which was great. Remember, I had three kids outside -- normally I can't even shower without being interrupted. As always in surrender -- I asked the Lord, "What do you want to give me in exchange?" He told me, "Authority, opportunity, the redemption of lost time, and lost dreams." It was a normal day, a regular moment that turned supernatural in seconds as the Lord invited me into an encounter to be engulfed in the fire of His presence that resulted in deeper passion and healing.

Why is this important you wonder? Oh, I am so happy you asked.

I want to be a prophetic voice for my generation and the ones to come. I had to get free from rejection so that I can stay in connection with the heart of God and keep my spiritual eyes and heart clean! I do not want to be a benchwarmer -- I want to play in the game! The fear of man, self-rejection, or even the fear of rejection will take you out of the game and put you onto the bench. And God never intended for there to be bench warmers in the Kingdom. **Galatians 1:10 (NIV)** says, "Am I now trying to win the approval of human beings, or of God? Or am I trying to please people? If I were still trying to please people, I would not be a servant of Christ." Fear and faith can not coexist in our thoughts just as a desire for men's and God's approval can't be housed in our hearts **(James 1:8)**.

REMEMBER THE RICH YOUNG MAN? He had great wealth. He wanted to be on the team and sit on the bench. He wanted to have his cake and eat it too. If we care about pleasing men, we will miss opportunities to please God and end up in sin. We have to say yes to one only. The fear of man will prove to be a snare **(Proverbs 29:25)** and while unintelligent, the enemy would love to ensnare us in a spirit of rejection. This is a perversion of the truth, a counterfeit way to live when God has given us a greater inheritance. In Ephesians 1, Paul writes what that inheritance is -- that we are blessed, chosen, loved, predestined, adopted, redeemed, forgiven, lavished with grace, included in Christ, sealed with the spirit and promised an inheritance. It says it right there -- we not only get to play, but we also get to be His burning ones on the winning team!

LOVE FEAST AND FIRES

> *FIRE FALLS ON SACRIFICE.*
> *Bill Johnson*

COUNT ZINZENDORF WAS BORN on the 26th of May,1700, in Dresden. He was a descendent of one of the most ancient noble families of the Archduchy of Austria. He was raised by his grandmother on her estate of Hennersdorf. After having finished his study of law in 1719, he traveled throughout Holland and France, giving his attention to the condition of the Church. He made the observation that to all these different denominations, one thing was common -- that true Christianity consisted in, "Christianity of the heart".

While visiting art galleries in Dusseldorf, he saw a painting of the crucifixion. Convicted by the words on the frame of the picture -- "All this I did for thee, What hast thou done for Me?" -- he gave his full yes to the Lord.

Returning from his travels, Zinzendorf undertook the management of his grandmother's estate. In 1722, Zinzendorf permitted some immigrants from Moravia who were attracted by the report of religious freedom to his estate in Berthelsdorf. This lasted a few years longer than expected as immigrants and refugees from many parts of Germany migrated to the Count's property. These refugees, called the Moravians, were taken in and fully cared for by the Count.

Upon arrival, the Moravians were a mess! They were judgmental, critical, and disunified. They couldn't get along with one another. They would fight over doctrine, over petty subjects, and stir up tension with one another. The issues escalated so much that Zinzendorf quit his career in law to manage the property, and the refugees on it, more effectively. He decided to go to their houses one-by-one to establish a healthy culture and a spirit of unity among his people. He would spend hours in conversation and conversion, encouraging them to repent for their judgmental hearts and leading them back to unity and love. He also gave each person a role based on their gifts so that everyone within the community had a purpose and the ability to add value to the culture.

As he went from home to home there came such a profound move of God, a love feast as they called it, that on August 13, 1727, about 100 refugees gathered all together to celebrate their renewed love for each other. The Holy Spirit fell in such a powerful way -- in strength and in power -- that a century later it was still referred to as the Moravians Pentecost. It changed the entire planet. Seven days after this "love feast" they entered into a 24-hour-day prayer that lasted for one hundred years without stopping. One hundred years of unending intercession and prayer which flowed through a moment of broken humble believers, and the world was never the same.

After the hundred years, they had a short break and then continued on for another twenty years of unending prayer and intercession. In August of 1732, two Moravians were chosen and sent out as the first missionaries from Herrnhut. They were followed by missionaries who were sent out to Greenland, Africa, South America, Asia, and America. Eventually, John Wesley would be born again through the ministry of a Moravian church in London. It was during these 120 years that the first and second great awakening was birthed; in later years, the slave trade was abolished in England through William Wilberforce.

Just before he died, Count Zinzendorf said to his son-in-law, "I am going to the Savior. I am ready. I am quite resigned to the will of my Lord. If He is no longer willing to make use of me here, I am quite ready to go to Him, for there is nothing more in my way".

We read in **Leviticus 9:24** how the fire of God fell upon the burnt offering and consumed it. That fire is a picture of the Holy Spirit which comes to consume our sacrifice, our prayers, our worship, our surrender. As priests unto the Lord, we get the wild opportunity to add fuel, wood, and kindling to the fire of our hearts and watch what God does. Count Zinzendorf is a great example of this. From one glance at a painting and the commission that came with the conviction, he devoted his life to the service and protection of immigrants. I can't prove it, but I don't believe he knew His devotion would lead to such selfless acts of love that would touch the entire world.

God doesn't require equal sacrifice, equal devotion, or equal surrender from His kids. The Lord has never asked me to open my home to refugees. The count longed to be in ministry yet had a profession in law. When the Lord called me to be a pastor I was more surprised than anyone else. I didn't want a role in the church, I wanted to be a stay-at-home mom. I remember the night I was asking Him if being a pastor was really his idea for my season. I was still trying to understand His plans. I asked Him, "What if I don't want to do it?" To which He gently responded, "Then you can be normal."

THE THOUGHT of being normal is no fun to me. It sounds boring and uneventful. The Lord knows I need adventure, new experiences, constant movement, and challenges. I stopped questioning the opportunity and assignment at that moment. I am so glad I did. The plans of the Lord are better than my greatest thoughts or dreams! I am more fulfilled (and tired) now than I ever have been and I wouldn't change a thing.

Jesus does unapologetically require our hearts, and He knows how to position us for both breakthrough and influence. He wired us from the beginning of time with gifts, talents, thought processes, and dreams. The more time we spend with Him, the clearer those are and the more familiar His voice becomes. It is when we develop our histories with Him, that He turns our mustard seeds of faith and small visions for our lives into movements that change the world.

WHEN WE LAY OUR LIFE DOWN FOR THE HEART OF THE KING, WE CAPTURE HIS PASSION AND FIND OUR DIVINE PURPOSE. TRUE GREATNESS IS ONLY FOUND AS WE DIE TO SELFISH AMBITION, JEALOUSY, ENVY, AND STRIFE, AND EMBRACE A NOBLE CULTURE THAT PROTECTS THE HEART OF THE KING. THERE IS NOTHING TOO NOBLE TO REACH FOR, TOO AWESOME TO BELIEVE FOR, TOO POWERFUL TO HOPE FOR, OR TOO EXCELLENT TO LIVE FOR, BECAUSE WE ARE THE CHILDREN OF THE KING.
Kris Vallotton

6

_____

FRIENDS OF GOD

*OUR ADVERSARY THE DEVIL MAJORS IN THREE THINGS:
NOISE, HURRY, AND CROWDS. IF HE CAN KEEP US INVOLVED
IN MUCHNESS AND MANYNESS HE WILL REST SATISFIED.*
Richard Foster

WE ENCOUNTER God in many different ways: obviously through reading His word, in church, in generosity, through community, in nature, through dreams and visions, worship, dance, art. Also, through journaling, meditating on scripture, soaking, or resting in the Lord.[12] The more time we spend with Jesus' in any of the ways above, the more emotionally mature we become. It takes time and practice -- that's why we are His disciples. We are learners of His heart and ways. But a disciple doesn't stop there -- we also practice what we learn.

It was fully God's intent to share a covenant relationship with us. We have been given the greatest thing in the world for free: the gift of His friendship. The trouble most Christians have is valuing His friendship for the gift it truly is. We communicate the values we are living into, through our behaviors and habits. It's a principle Jesus shared with us years ago -- wherever your treasure is your heart is **(Matthew 6:21)**. We build a history with God when we choose to value our friendship with Him.

The resurrection of Jesus Christ as well as the opportunity of having a friendship with Him is what distinguishes us from every other religion in the world. Not only do we serve a God who is alive but we serve a God who wants to be our friend. This is straight from the heart of God as Jesus Himself said:

> So this is my command: Love each other deeply, as much as I have loved you. For the greatest love of all is a love that sacrifices all. And this great love is demonstrated when a person sacrifices his life for his friends. You show that you are My intimate friends when you obey all that I command you.
>
> I have never called you 'servants,' because a master doesn't confide in his servants, and servants don't always understand what the master is doing. But I call you My most intimate friends, for I reveal to you everything that I've heard from My Father.

John 15:12- 15 (TPT)

What makes a good friend? How important is it to you to be known and understood? Friends bond with each other in crisis moments, life experiences, and new opportunities. Good friends remember these moments, are good listeners, and discern what makes each other tick. They are silly; they don't pretend to be something they are not. Good friends finish each other's sentences because they know each other so well! Good friends know the sound of your voice and exactly what you mean when you text certain emojis or gifs.

When my youngest son Luke was seven, we were out on a hang out (I'm not allowed to call these times dates). As he was eating his frozen yogurt, I asked Luke what he loves about Ethan, his brother. He said, "I love that Ethan always says he is sorry when he hurts me." I thought about how brilliant and mature His response was. His little heart knows he is safe with his brother because Ethan repents when he is wrong and violates his trust. It would be so normal for a kid at that age to reply with, "He is funny" or "He has really good ideas!" However, the deeper need of our hearts is to feel safe with our friends. This made me think about being a friend of God's, and what my responsibility is in protecting His heart.

I want God to feel safe with me. I want to be able to treat His heart with the care that He deserves and when I've hurt Him apologize quickly. My preference, my will, my agenda is not as important as His heart is to me! I also want God to speak into my processes and growth. I want to know what He is thinking and adjust my decisions with His needs and desires in mind. God even models this type of friendship with us! Let's look at His friendship Abraham:

When the men got up to leave, they looked down toward Sodom, and Abraham walked along with them to see them on their way. Then the Lord said, "Shall I hide from Abraham what I am about to do? Abraham will surely become a great and powerful nation, and all nations on Earth will be blessed through him. For I have chosen him, so that he will direct his children and his household after him to keep the way of the Lord by doing what is right and just, so that the Lord will bring about for Abraham what He has promised him."

Then the Lord said, "The outcry against Sodom and Gomorrah is so great and their sin so grievous that I will go down and see if what they have done is as bad as the outcry that has reached me. If not, I will know."

The men turned away and went toward Sodom, but Abraham remained standing before the Lord. Then Abraham approached him and said: "Will you sweep away the righteous with the wicked? What if there are fifty righteous people in the city? Will you really sweep it away and not spare the place for the sake of the fifty righteous people in it? Far be it from you to do such a thing—to kill the righteous with the wicked, treating the righteous and the wicked alike. Far be it from you! Will not the Judge of all the Earth do right?"

The Lord said, "If I find fifty righteous people in the city of Sodom, I will spare the whole place for their sake."

Then Abraham spoke up again: "Now that I have been so bold as to speak to the Lord, though I am nothing but dust and ashes, what if the number of the righteous is five less than fifty? Will you destroy the whole city for lack of five people?"

"If I find forty-five there," he said, "I will not destroy it."

Once again he spoke to Him, "What if only forty are found there?"

He said, "For the sake of forty, I will not do it."

Then he said, "May the Lord not be angry, but let me speak. What if only thirty can be found there?"

He answered, "I will not do it if I find thirty there."

Abraham said, "Now that I have been so bold as to speak to the Lord, what if only twenty can be found there?"

He said, "For the sake of twenty, I will not destroy it."

Then he said, "May the Lord not be angry, but let me speak just once more. What if only ten can be found there?"

He answered, "For the sake of ten, I will not destroy it."

When the Lord had finished speaking with Abraham, he left, and Abraham returned home.

Genesis 18:16-33 (NIV)

You can argue that Yahweh didn't intend to destroy the city and this was a test. But I think this text shows us a glimpse of God's heart as it pertains to His desire for friendship and communion with us. Built inside relationships is the need for give and take -- the converging of two beings who are willing to submit to the other for pleasure and connection. One of the most basic psychological needs of humanity is connection. This is because we are wired for love, made in the image of God who is love, and also invented connection. He is not so attached to His will, way, or agenda that He is immovable or not willing to participate in give and take in our relationship. (We will share more in-depth about this later!)

During services at church, I will often receive a text from a good friend who asks, "Are you here? I thought I heard you!" Every time I read that text it makes me feel known! Now, I tend to be a loud person. I'm loud in church because I am so passionate about Jesus! When I'm in a room, it is more uncommon that you do not hear a "Come on!", "Amen!" or "So good!" But we attend a megachurch, and at any service, there are at least 350 people in the Worship Center, and I am not the only one excited about Jesus!

My friends know me so well they can pick my voice out of a crowd. What a mark of true friendship -- that you can pick out the sound of your friend's voice when 350 people are present. In order to be able to do that you have to spend a sufficient amount of time with that friend. The Lord used this to speak to me years ago. I found myself wondering, "Have I spent enough time with Jesus that I can pick His voice out in a crowd? Do I know Him well enough to pick out the color, tone, and intonation of his voice when I am in the midst of hundreds of others?"

These are convicting questions. Our heart is where our treasure is (Matthew 6:33). I want my treasure to be Jesus and my heart to be as close to Him as possible. This means I not only keep the fire burning on my heart but that I lean into His voice and friendship to build connectedness with Him. Again, it is in this place where we build our history with God. My history with Him is the most precious thing that I have. More than furniture, possessions, money in the bank, and this book, the moments I have shared with the Lord, the face-to-face encounters with Him are my prized treasures!

HOW CAN WE HAVE REVIVAL WHEN WE VALUE A BOOK THE
EARLY CHURCH DIDN'T HAVE OVER THE HOLY SPIRIT THEY
DID HAVE?
Kris Vallotton

BUILDING A HISTORY WITH GOD

IF YOU MAKE HISTORY WITH GOD, HE WILL CHANGE HISTORY
THROUGH YOU.
Bill Johnson

THERE ARE multiple benefits to cultivating our friendships with God. When we keep track of our history and experiences with God, it gives people permission and faith to experience the same level or depth of intimacy with Him as well. It's what I expect to happen to you as you read this book. But that is not why I set out to create and share my history with Him. It was not so I could write a book. It also wasn't so I could preach a message. It's so you and I have authority over the message we carry. A message and a book may come out of your history with the Lord, but it's not the reason we do it!

When I started devoting the time to writing down my encounters with the Lord they increased. The Lord told me that the discipline I was practicing showed Him I valued the encounters I was experiencing. I was developing faithfulness as I stewarded His voice. I want to be accountable to what He says and the revelation He gives me. He trusts me with His heart, His voice, and His people and I believe it started years ago on a blank page.

There are so many great benefits to intentionally developing a friendship with God. However, here is a shortlist with some personal examples from the pages of my journal:

1. Intimacy comes out of friendship.

Intimacy with God happens in small moments over long periods of time by simply choosing to be with Him. It is what we were made for. God is in the big things just as much as He is in the small. Don't miss what is behind a small moment or a small sacrifice. Often, the most profound encounters come from a casual invitation from the Lord that we could have easily disregarded. Because He created us with a need for Him, He satisfies us and fills us up when we spend time with Him.[13]

Years, ago I was soaking with the Lord, I thought about how the Lord who created the entire universe, who is matchless in glory, wisdom, and honor is the same God who is referred to as the Lifter of our heads **(Psalms 3:3)**. I asked Him why He wanted to be the one to lift our heads? I was curious, why not leave that opportunity to our community, our family, servants, pastors, or slaves? He told me, "Because I want to be the one who locks eyes with My kids. I want to be the first thing they see!"

Another day, I was soaking after reading the Sermon on the Mount. Using my imagination, I pictured myself being there. I told Jesus I wanted to follow Him around while He was teaching and healing the crowd. Instantly He picked me up and we started walking up to the Mount of Olives. I told Him He didn't have to carry me the entire way (independent even in my imagination) and He insisted. He smiled and said, "Trust me, these crowds can get crazy." He squeezed me and I asked if He missed walking around on Earth with us. He said, "Yes, I do, I loved being so close to my kids and sharing moments with them. Sometimes I still come down and walk among you because I long to be so close to you all. Even if my people don't notice it, this is what My heart longs for."

2. It's where we are taught by the Spirit of God Himself.

We learn our identity from Jesus. Yes, we can read books, listen to podcasts and TED talks, have an awesome pastor that preaches well -- but we learn our identities through friendship with God and revelation from God. In building a friendship and history with Him, you have documented proof (if you write it down) of the testimony of God's goodness, His plans, faithfulness, and power specifically in your life. This builds faith and trust in our friendship; matures us, and gives us a purpose or vision for our destiny.

We learn how to strengthen ourselves in the Lord in the alone moments with God. When David was abandoned by everyone whether they loved him or hated him -- he turned to the Lord to build him up **(1 Samuel 30:6)**.[14] The voice of the Lord should always be the loudest influence in our belief system.

Also, when the enemy comes to try to lie to us **(John 10:10)** about our purpose and influence, we have proof that he is wrong. So many times when I have been under attack in my mind, when I have felt hopeless about my destiny, I will read my history to the devil. It's a great way to fight! I was born to terrorize the enemy and wear him out. He eventually leaves because he hates to be reminded of the deposit God made inside of me and the impact for the Kingdom I have.

The Lord taught me about His desire to partner with us through a vision He showed me. I saw both developed and underdeveloped land in this picture in my mind. The people all around were going about their business. Jesus gave me a scarf of many colors. It was long and flowing. As I moved with it, kids came running up to me to play dance with it. I went through a door and it led to the same place but on this side, everyone was working together to better their land, businesses, community, and society. God was there with me. I didn't understand exactly how, but I knew I had something to do with the improvement and wholeness in the culture. I turned to Him and said, "Wow, You look like Your son." He replied. "So do you." I was so taken aback and astonished I opened my eyes pulling my focus off the vision. He trusts me! He was teaching me that cultural transformation is fun and easy. I sat stunned at what I heard and saw. I couldn't believe the Lord thinks I look like His son and prefers me to be used by Him to bring healing and change to the world.

3. It is where we receive strategy for our life.

Strategic insight and wisdom are more available for us than we know. In my imagination there are trees in heaven and the fruit that grows on those trees is wisdom, strategy, insight, understanding, language, foresight, etc. When we ask for these abilities **(James 1:5)**, the Lord gives them! He is a good Dad. He can't hold back giving to His kids what they need! When we sit and wait on Him **(Psalms 27:13)**, He shows up and He shows off!

Years ago when my kids were nine, four, and three, I remember crying out to the Lord for help. (Yes, you -- mom with the Cheerios in your hair -- you are not alone, you will sleep again one day). I was at the end of my rope- tired, impatient, and scared. Instantly in my mind, I saw Jesus and I playing, laughing, and dancing. He was not stressed out like I was. I was confused about why He was not using that moment to teach me some 'spiritual principle' or override my will with supernatural patience so I didn't hurt one of them! I asked Him why He was revealing Himself to me that way and He said, "I come to you with playing, singing, dancing, and laughing because this is what you are doing now. The strategies will come when you need them. Family is what we are doing now and this is what you need. You need the intimate, silly side of me. Remember our goal is connection. This is why we dance. When we dance, you feel free. Carry that freedom into your home. Kids who experience freedom thrive. Here is your strategy: play! This is how I build a house **(Psalm 127)**. You are doing well. Trust me, you'll have everything when you need it." It was a game-changer for me and a strategy that I still use as a parent!

Another time, while I was resting, actually I was laying out in the sun hoping to get tan! The Lord showed me a new season of operation. He was my coach and I was a runner. We were preparing for a race. He was whispering to me before the race started, "Remember what I've taught you -- this is a strategic race. What you do at ALL times matters. Remember My voice, remember our training. Remember how you have felt. You can win this but you have to listen to Me." I felt in the encounter that I was well supported and well trained. I didn't feel the voice of the Lord came as a warning or a threat. He had already positioned and taught me to run. It was my responsibility to heed His advice and trust in Him and in my training. It was strategic and intentional. Apparently, I've trained for whatever is next!

A few years later when I had the opportunity to take a new position at my church and it was a confusing time for me to evaluate where my energy should go. I asked Him for help, and He replied, "If you champion love, I will take care of the rest. It is the only strategy you need. Follow love, be loved, increase in love. We've got this!"

4. It gives us opportunities for reflection, remembrance, and revelation.

Psalms 105:5 (NIV) says, "Remember the wonders He has done, His miracles." **Psalm 77:11 (NIV)** says, "I will remember the deeds of the Lord, yes, I will remember the miracles of long ago." Maybe it's mom-brain, maybe it's pastor-brain, but I forget things all the time. My kids hate it. I hate it too! If I don't write something down, I forget it. If you tell me a story while I am multitasking, typing, or tired I ain't gonna remember. It's not just facts that I forget -- I am horrible with dates, names, and remembering testimonies unless I write things down.

We overcome and build faith through recounting testimonies **(Revelation 12:11)**. When we feed ourselves on the testimonies of what God is doing we will not be overcome by discouragement. I want to be a carrier of hope! It is easy for me to have hope for other people. However, for myself and my family... it is more difficult at times. So I've learned to use the pages of my journal to challenge the spirit of discouragement by reminding myself and the demonic spirit of the testimonies of God. When I've been believing by faith for a breakthrough for a long time but haven't had an answer, this is how I take heart **(John 16:33)**. I read through the times and ways God has shown up in my past and release the stories and testimonies over myself to build up my faith.

At its core, testimony means, "Do it again." Testimony is powerful for all the reasons I've listed above and more because when we share testimonies, we activate personal and corporate faith in ourselves and others to believe God to DO IT AGAIN!!

I taught kids ministry for years. I always tried to find ways to make the Bible come alive, not just teach a story. I wanted to show our preschool kids the power of what testimony means. So I told them of course it means we are yelling up to heaven for God to do it again. To build boldness and connective tissue with our three and four-year-olds, I would blow bubbles and then instruct them to shout out, "DO IT AGAIN, DO IT AGAIN!!" Can you hear the chant of the preschoolers in your imagination? After the kids were familiar with the cadence and joy attached to the language, we used this chant every time we would share miracles of what God had done or what He did do, from Moses parting the Red Sea to Jesus healing Conner's boo-boo, we would call on God to DO IT AGAIN!!

5. Our history becomes the foundation for the next generation's faith.

I refuse for there to be a generation that comes after me that does not know God or His deeds **(Judges 2:10)**. This is one reason why we must remember! I take the time to write and document my history so there will be proof of the goodness of God on the Earth **(Psalm 78:4)**. I keep history journals for my kids as well so when they tell me, "I don't hear God speak to me", or when they go through doubt and unbelief, we can read through the pages of their encounters with Him.

When my son, Ethan, was seven years old he had a nasty scab on his hand. One day, as it was healing, it fell off to reveal a scar. He asked Jesus what He thought of his hand and ran downstairs to tell me, Jesus said, "I don't see anything. It's perfect." He was smiling from ear to ear. "Why are you so happy about that bud?" I asked him. "Because Jesus doesn't see my mistakes." He ran off and I sat there stunned. I didn't know if he was struggling in that area or what the Lord was doing but I was so proud that my son was nurturing his own friendship with the Lord.

Years ago, I heard Bill Johnson talk about being a friend of God and what he would advise people to do if that was what they were seeking to build. His advice was, "Grow in your affection for Him. The willingness to spend time with Him without asking for anything and stop evaluating yourself. If you can't, you will live with an awareness of what doesn't work and what is not right as you disqualify His significance for you." Go ahead, read that again, I know it's so good! Since hearing that, I've made his advice a part of my spiritual practice. Many of my friendship moments with Jesus are in silence simply growing in affection for each other.

This is the prize of my life, the reason I exist, to call myself His friend as well as for Him to call me His friend in return. I don't want to be buried, but if I had to be and had a tombstone, I wouldn't want it to say, "Christina Andriese, best pastor who lived," or "Christina Andriese, great mom, great wife". I want to be a good pastor, a great mom, and a great wife -- but that's not what I burn for. It would however, be the highest honor if it said something like what James said about Abraham (James 2:23): "Christina Andriese, Jesus' best friend."

THE FIRST AND PRIMARY BUSINESS TO
WHICH I OUGHT TO ATTEND EVERY DAY IS TO HAVE
MY SOUL HAPPY IN THE LORD.
George Mueller

7

BORN FOR SIGNIFICANCE

*IF I MISDIAGNOSE WHO A PERSON IS AND THEIR PLACE
BEFORE GOD I WILL MISTREAT THEM. EVERY PERSON IS
SIGNIFICANT IN GOD'S EYES AND THEREFORE
MUST BECOME SO IN OURS.*
Bill Johnson

IN 1703, a hero was born who changed history. From the time that John Wesley's heart would be "strangely warmed" to his dying day, he never stopped his tireless work of releasing reformation and revival. This encounter so marked him that he started a movement focused on deep devotion through the spiritual disciplines, as well as great servitude to the poor and lost. He would travel on horseback from town to town preaching the kingdom of God. It is estimated that he rode 250,000 miles in his lifetime and delivered over 45,000 messages on the good news of Jesus Christ.

Out of his mentorship and commissioning arose Francis Asbury who some historians said outrode Wesley once he came to America. It is recorded that he spent more miles on a horse than any man in history. Though Wesley was the father of Methodism, Asbury would be credited for recruiting and organizing a band of selfless and radical Christians called the Circuit Riders, who launched America into what we now identify in church history as the First Great Awakening. When Asbury arrived in America, there were a few hundred Methodists and a few dozen preachers, but by the time he died, there were over 210,000 followers of Jesus and over 4,000 preachers.

The Circuit Riders traveled the frontiers of America for decades, taking the Gospel to the most remote places in America. In a time of American history where it was easier to stay in one place and live in the comfort of the few cities that existed, these men refused comfort and chose to be sanctified and zealous. Over half of them died before reaching age 33 and their annual pay, if any, was around 50 dollars. They were changed by their own encounters with the Lord that led them to live out their passion which was to see every home in America hear and believe the Gospel. History was changed forever because these brave and wild men shared a history with the Lord.

We've already established the fire of God in your life is your responsibility to maintain. But we don't do it so we can burn for other people, to draw a crowd, or build a social media platform. We maintain our relationship with Him because this is where the fullness of life is! I'm sure (though I haven't heard it from them personally... that would be weird) that Wesley and Asbury weren't concerned about what we were going to Google about them one day or their names being printed in books. They were burning and had to live out the call of God on their life. Their devotion wasn't to become famous -- it was to see the lost saved.

We don't know what it cost them. We can imagine the sacrifice, but we can't really know what their surrender and worship did for Jesus or for themselves. But I do believe that they lived the principles in this book, and you and I are invited to do the same.

EVERYONE WHO SPENT TIME WITH JESUS BEGAN TO DREAM
OF SIGNIFICANCE.
Bill Johnson

A FEW YEARS AGO, when my daughter was in elementary school, we watched a documentary on one of our nation's heroes, Martin Luther King Jr. She had been studying his life and impact in her social studies class. As we started the show, I asked her, "What have you learned so far?" A quick reply came, "That he did good things and stood up for what was right."

After the documentary finished, our conversation dove deeper than second-grade history. I tried to explain to her that anyone could have done what MLK did if they choose to listen to their heart and not be afraid. Anyone could have had the same impact and influence. To this, she replied, "Yeah, he was nothing special."

I sat back in my seat stunned. "Did I somehow imply that he wasn't special?" I thought to myself. Had I lost control of the conversation? Let's be real, it wouldn't be the first time! Then the Lord hit me with the truth. (You know the moment you have a thought that was way better than you could have come up with on your own!)

I told her, "No, babe, he was special. Everyone is special. Everyone was created to stand up for love, righteousness, and justice. Everyone has a destiny to do something impossible for God. It is just that only some people actually accomplish their destiny. Very few people make the choice to live in complete surrender to God. Few people believe God enough to refuse to allow fear to hold them back from pursuing God's destiny for them."

Her attention was captured, the light bulb turned on, and she understood. The funny thing, I finally understood something too. Greatness has been placed inside every one of us. Each one of us was born to partner with Jesus to change the world and release His heart. It is in His heart to communicate to all of humanity that we all deserve dignity, value, and honor no matter what color our skin is, where we live, or what we do.

I heard Pastor Bill Johnson, from Bethel Church, share some insight on raising his kids. When he tucked them into bed at night, he would ask his children to inquire of the Lord, "What impossible assignment have you created me for?" I've done this a few times with my babies, but I can't pray it over my kids unless I also believe it for myself.

> *THERE ARE THREE STAGES TO EVERY GREAT*
> *WORK OF GOD; FIRST IS THE IMPOSSIBLE,*
> *THEN IT IS DIFFICULT, THEN IT IS DONE.*
> *J. Hudson Taylor*

Since Jesus' time on Earth, each generation has struggled to understand the fullness of what it looks like to be the Bride of Christ. Even with the continual unveiling of more revelation as time goes on, the bride has remained confused about her destiny. This often happens when one generation believes an extreme version of the truth and then the next generation creates a belief system in response to that extreme -- which can be just as extreme! Extreme is not synonymous with truth, and truth is what we are going after! The good news is -- truth has a name -- His name is Jesus!

Significance is an example of one of those concepts that can cause confusion and a reactionary belief system. Significance and success are not synonymous. I am not talking about success; I am talking about our destiny. Clay Scroggins says it like this in his book, How to Lead When You're Not in Charge, "We were all created to thirst for purpose. What you believe about why you're on Earth will deeply affect the opportunities you see available to you and how you should capitalize on them with your time, gifts, talents, and energy."

Ephesians 2:10 tells us we are born to do great things that God had actually set into motion before He set us into motion. To do "great things" often requires a great leader, a great learner, a great communicator, or a great builder. Our significance and worth are not derived from our gifts or talents or time-management skills! Our significance is attached to the worthiness of Christ, of the value of knowing Christ, of being known by Christ, of being in Christ, and of preaching Christ.

Again I want to be clear -- I am not talking about success, achievements, performance, or platforms. I'm talking about Jesus getting the full reward for what He paid to redeem our souls by us living with an internal burning to be transformed to look like Him. It is equally important that we do not let our physical achievements define us. In her book So-Called Genius, Laura Fraser writes, "If your identity is wrapped in the magnificent things you're destined to achieve – as a great writer, musician, scientist, politician, chef -- the thought you might produce something mediocre can be devastating."

Our purposes are not intended to devastate us. When people pursue positions and achievements, they end up being defined by them. But if you pursue passion and intimacy with Jesus, then when you have a position you end up defining it -- not being defined by it. The Lord wants us to be identified by who we are becoming, not by what we are accomplishing.

The truth is that significance, greatness, potential, whatever you want to call it is just as much a part of your DNA as your eye color, your blood type, and your sex drive. This can be damaging under a false need for success, or empowering under a God-ordained desire for amazing kids! We are made in the image of God who is the originator of greatness, great things, and great kids. The focus shouldn't be on what we produce, it should be on who we are magnifying **(Matthew 5:16)**.

If we were to be honest, our discomfort with this conversation comes from one of two places. First, from seeing it modeled inappropriately and someone operating out of their significance which leads to the exploitation of people, or second, our fear of our own pride.

Both are ugly and not of God. Those are perversions of the truth, a different version. But it doesn't mean that the truth is less true. Make sense? We can not reduce the truth because we are scared of how we can mess things up. If we did that, so much of the dreams of God's heart and His plan for His family wouldn't happen.

Believing in a Sovereign God invokes participation as His bride. If we believe God Himself is supreme and all that matters, then we are also believing that His people's choices do not matter. Have you ever had this thought: "God is so vast He will accomplish His will with me or without me." Or heard people say, "God is going to do what He wants to do one way or another. God is in control, He is in charge." There is an aspect of that which is true, however not all things are His plans or under His approval. There are two wills of God: the things we can not change, such as Jesus coming back **(1 Thessalonians 4:16, John 14:3)** and the things we can change, His will that no one would die without knowing Him **(2 Peter 3:9)**.

We have a vital part to play. We cannot adapt to such an extreme view of His sovereignty because it takes away our responsibilities. Consider what generations are limited in accomplishing when they believe in extremes! Father God is like a father who invites his young kid to help him repair a car. The father knows that the teaching, training, and timing will produce a different outcome than if he did it alone, yet He still brings his kid in because He values the partnership and learning process. He would rather do it with us and not have things be perfect than do it without us.

God made Himself vulnerable to the impact and choices of His people when He chose to co-labor with us. This takes us back to our conversation about God and Abraham and their friendship. The give and take that comes with connection is a wild thought! He can do everything so much better without us, yet He put a plan in place where we would be the ones that would make Earth like heaven. This was His original design and plan -- co-laboring with us was and is His plan 'A' **(1 Corinthians 9:3)**.

If it's true (which it is, wink wink) that there is an exchange in the presence of God that leads to a transformation of our lives -- then His will becomes our will and vice versa. Not every option we have is inspired by the Lord. Choice means freedom and sometimes an option will be presented to us that tests what is in our hearts. This provides us with opportunities to see the motives of our own hearts. For example, David was prophesied he would have the opportunity to kill King Saul, but when the time arose he said, "I know better than to kill the Lord's appointed" **(1 Samuel 24:6)**. David passed this test of opportunity because he was not driven by a motive to become King; he was driven by a heart that pleased God.

When we are mature in the Lord and healthy, we do not have to fear the destiny God has given us! I have never self-promoted. I've never applied for a position or written a resume to serve Jesus. I'm also not saying those things are wrong. I've never built a public figure social media page. I don't even have listed on my social media that I am a pastor. I'm not identified by those things. I am identified by who I am becoming, and that's how I can pursue a life of significance! The opportunist mentality isn't often the way of the kingdom. Self-promotion is exhausting and whatever we build through our own strength and a desire for promotion, we have to sustain through our own efforts. However, when we build under grace, then the Lord sustains us and our efforts and turns them into a legacy! That is what I want. This is the way of the revivalist.

AS OUR HEARTS BECOME PURE, OUR
VISION BECOMES CLEARER.
Heidi Baker

PERMISSION TO FAIL

SUCCESS IS MOVING FROM FAILURE TO FAILURE
WITHOUT LOSS OF ENTHUSIASM.
Winston Churchill

SINCE GOD WANTS all of his kids running around the world representing Him, He has built messes and failure into the equation. That means God expects that we will blow it! I am not even talking about sin, I am talking about mistakes and messes. As we are living as burning flames of His love, things will get burned! Isn't that freeing? I don't have to be scared of my greatness or my failures! I just have to be willing to grow.

Years ago, my sister Andrea and I were on our way to visit our friends at the women's California Department of Corrections and Rehabilitation Camp. It is more commonly referred to as a "fire camp," since the majority of the work the inmates do is fighting and helping to prevent wildfires while they serve their time in California. These gals are bad A$$!!

It was December and we were going to share a message about Jesus and Christmas. I was praying so seriously on the drive out to the facility: "Lord let them encounter You! God would You please show up! Help me with my mouth so I don't say anything stupid, we want to represent You so well!" I was in serious intercession mode, praying all the right things with a spirit of heaviness and seriousness. My brilliant sister saw how serious I was and interrupted me. "This isn't going to be hard. We don't have to worry about representing Him we just get to re-present Him!"

It took me a while to understand what she was saying. I was so caught up in my desire not to screw up I couldn't connect the dots at first. Re-present Him? It was so simple. Jesus Christ has already done everything. I was just being asked to deliver Him as a present to His daughters! I could do that! Maybe since it was Christmas it was the perfect language I needed to unlock my fear and lean into my yes of being in the same way with Him by re-gifting Him!

The lifestyle of a revivalist is all about obeying God and serving His family in love. It is that simple. I enjoy activating people to take risks, make mistakes, clean up their messes, celebrate their victories, and go out to do it all again. I always make sure that if I ask someone to take a risk I do it first. Since there is no fear in love there is no fear in risks, but I am not merciless! I think it is only fair when I am putting people through so much discomfort! But I have learned that discomfort only lasts eight seconds and if I can surrender the eight seconds, I will see miracles!

Here is a response from one of my students when I asked her to write about her risk journey. Maybe you will hear your voice in her words.

On the last day of 2019, the Lord spoke to me telling me that among other things, this year would be the year of "taking risks with excitement and laughing at failure." As uncomfortable as this sounded, I also knew that letting uncomfortable become my new comfortable was something I had felt pulled to start. I decided to make taking risks my new norm, and am practicing quick obedience when I feel the Lord is speaking to me.

A few weeks back, my aunt came to visit with her son and my family sat them down to pray for her upcoming surgery. She shared tearfully that she wasn't sure if she would make it out of this one. She had many health issues that kept her in bondage, for as long as I could remember. She also carried a great deal of heaviness in relation to her family, as her husband suffers from severe chronic depression, her son with autism, and her mother with schizophrenia and other mental illnesses.

I got a vision of a beautiful butterfly and the word "lightness." The prayer closed, and although she is a Christian, I hesitated to tell her, wondering if she was comfortable with the prophetic. I decided, whether she thought I was crazy or not, she needed to know the Fathers' heart for her, and that this heaviness was not His best for her.

As I was explaining the vision to her, my sister stood up and said she saw butterflies as we were praying too. As my aunt cried, she received the word and interpretation, and she left to have her surgery.

A new thought came into my mind. It is only in risk that we understand the Father's heart for others. We can hear His voice over and over, telling us His love for us, but until we love the world with His words in moments of risk, we will never love the world with His heart.

The reward to risk is incredible. In all my years being in the same way with Jesus, I have observed more breakthroughs and fruit in people's lives when they practice risk. God wants to give you the desires of your heart, but He also wants you to fulfill the desires of His heart. You have a divine destiny. There is a reason why you are alive at this time in history. We have been called to be people of greatness. You were born to be amazing. God made us this way. The gifts and talents God has placed inside every human being are what brings Him great joy. What we do with them is up to us.

GOD WILL FULFILL ALL OF HIS PROMISES BUT HE IS NOT
OBLIGATED TO FULFILL YOUR POTENTIAL.
Larry Randolph

HIDDEN IN OBSCURITY

MOSES SPENT FORTY YEARS IN THE KING'S PALACE THINKING
THAT HE WAS SOMEBODY; THEN HE LIVED FORTY YEARS IN
THE WILDERNESS FINDING OUT THAT WITHOUT GOD HE WAS
A NOBODY; FINALLY, HE SPENT FORTY MORE YEARS
DISCOVERING HOW A NOBODY WITH GOD CAN BE A
SOMEBODY.
Dwight L. Moody

Let's recap a bit of what we have even learned so far on our journey together.

In our relationship with the Lord, there is an exchange that happens in His presence, and it shapes our passions and dreams. As we encounter

Him, we receive authority and the commissioning for our assignments. The more we build our history with the Lord, the stronger our friendship becomes, the more our hearts ache to see Earth become like heaven. The more we operate in purity and power, the more we connect to our original design of significance! This is God's intention - - a bride that is spotless, blameless, and fit for His son, Jesus!

My boys are weird when it comes to food. They have no grid for control other than their taste buds. They will shamelessly lie straight to my face to get out of eating something they hate. I'm for real -- no shame, no fear of discipline, no sorrow for breaking my heart. They will lie, lie, and lie again, to avoid a veggie or oddly textured food. On the other hand, they will eat past the point of pain if something tastes good. We can see it on their face and in their body language. They will be hunched over, glassy-eyed, burping, and still ask for another breadstick at Olive Garden just to lick the butter off the top.

Before we can manage our appetite, we have to acknowledge that we have one! This is another reason why this conversation is so important. We were born to carry and release revival. We are revivalists who are each significant. We need to be able to say that we hunger and long to fulfill the greatness God has placed inside of us. John Maxwell says, "Your potential is God's gift to you, what you do with it is your gift to Him."

Then what does a healthy desire for significance look like? Who have you seen model it well?

The antidote to an inappropriate desire for significance is the fruit of the Spirit of God in our lives. I've heard many pastors and leaders from Bethel Church simplify it with this phrase: purity plus power. The fruit of the Spirit is the character of God in us. The gift of the Spirit is the power of God at work in us. The anointing is the Holy Spirit building His character into us so we can operate in the fullness of His power, which is released through the gifts of the Holy Spirit. We corrupt the power of God without the character (fruit) of the Holy Spirit. The fruit of the Spirit should be at the core of who we are. As God transforms our character into His character, then He releases more of His gifts into us.

God has called you to be the answer to your dysfunctional family. You are the answer to the brokenness in the world; you are the answer to the corruption in government; you are the answer to the injustice in the medical field; you are the answer to the cries of the world around you. You were born to revive dead things, find lost things, and renew old things. You were created for good works long before sin was established on Earth and good works were needed.

Scripture is filled with examples of people who followed Yahweh or Jesus and were taken out of the public view and into a hidden place before they could destroy or abort their destinies. Obscurity. It's a funny thing -- the state of being unknown. It's so contradictory to the western culture where kids are getting phones and social media at ten years old. But what if…. What if obscurity is a missing link to doing the Christian life well? Or to finish our race well? Think through some of the major biblical players and their history with God. What happened in their years of obscurity?

We have the apostle Paul who in **Galatians 1** writes about his time in obscurity:

I was advancing in Judaism beyond many of my own age among my people and was extremely zealous for the traditions of my fathers. But when God, who set me apart from my mother's womb and called me by His grace, was pleased to reveal His Son in me so that I might preach Him among the Gentiles, my immediate response was not to consult any human being. I did not go up to Jerusalem to see those who were apostles before I was, but I went into Arabia. Later I returned to Damascus. Then after three years, I went up to Jerusalem to get acquainted with Cephas and stayed with him fifteen days. I saw none of the other apostles—only James, the Lord's brother. I assure you before God that what I am writing you is no lie. **Galatians 1:14-20 (NIV)**

He didn't get saved and then a microphone. He didn't get healed then turned around and prayed for someone's healing. Most likely it was during those three years that the Lord began to reveal to Paul many deep spiritual truths. Paul started his friendship with Jesus in obscurity. They were not wasted years, but years of preparation so that when he was given the opportunity to speak, he would have the authority, power, and fruit to teach from.

I like Paul because he chose to be led by the Lord into hiddenness and obscurity -- unlike Joseph, another one of my heroes, who I find myself relating to more. Joe was a spoiled brat. He knew he was his father's favorite and like my youngest got away with all the last-born stuff. He was gifted and unrefined. Prideful and immature. To protect Joseph's calling, the Lord stepped in! The Lord used the circumstances in his life to bring character like honor, humility, wisdom, understanding, empathy into Joseph's personality. Yahweh didn't take away Joseph's calling but worked the kinks out of his character in slave quarters and a jail cell. **(Genesis 39-41)**

There are many more from Jesus' life, and He Himself spent ninety percent of His own time on Earth in obscurity, where He overcame temptation and opposition **(Matthew 4:1-11)** and learned how to narrow His focus to what His heavenly Father was doing **(John 5:19)**. Moses learned the tension between justice and righteousness while hiding in the desert **(Exodus 2-6)**. And then we have Mary, Jesus' mother, who learned how to steward favor in the secret place **(Luke 1:26-56)**. This has also been much of my story.

DON'T THINK LESS OF YOURSELF BUT THINK ABOUT
YOURSELF LESS.
C.S. Lewis

A FEW YEARS AGO, I was given the most amazing opportunity to be our church's Children's Ministry Director. One of the great privileges of my life! It wasn't something I had ever been given a prophetic word about. I didn't go to school to sharpen my ability to lead in this role. Honestly, I had no idea what I was doing. We had between four to five hundred kids in our ministry any given weekend. Five services a week, over two hundred team members, and I was leading a staff of over thirty people.

Up until that time I had worked as a server, barista, and hairdresser. Jesus is fun! The Lord was with me, gave me an amazing team, and taught me quickly! People asked after a few months of my success if I had prophetic words to prepare me for this opportunity. Because I keep track of all my prophetic words (now), I looked back to check. A children's ministry director role wasn't ever spoken in any of my prophetic words, however, the words that I received years ago about what the Lord had in store for me brought me to a place of evaluating my character, pursuing self-discipline, and developing my gifts while I was hidden so when the day of favor and promotion came I was ready.

The prophetic words helped me position my life for something God wanted to do in and through me. This anointing, the ability to lead a team, and manage a ministry area this large wasn't birthed from a supernatural encounter. It came out of spending years serving someone else's vision, spending time with the Lord when no one was looking, and slowly growing in faithfulness and friendship.

Similarly, before David was a king, a warrior, or a public figure, he was hidden in the fields caring for his father's sheep.

> David said to Saul, "Let no one lose heart on account of this Philistine; your servant will go and fight him." Saul replied, "You are not able to go out against this Philistine and fight him; you are only a young man, and he has been a warrior from his youth."

> But David said to Saul, "Your servant has been keeping his father's sheep. When a lion or a bear came and carried off a sheep from the flock, I went after it, struck it and rescued the sheep from its mouth. When it turned on me, I seized it by its hair, struck it and killed it. Your servant has killed both the lion and the bear; this uncircumcised

Philistine will be like one of them, because he has defied the armies of the living God. The Lord who rescued me from the paw of the lion and the paw of the bear will rescue me from the hand of this Philistine." Saul said to David, "Go, and the Lord be with you."

1 Samuel 17:32-37 (NIV)

I wonder if in this moment, David connected the dots. I can imagine him chuckling as he was listening to Saul and whispering to the Lord, "Ah, now I see what you've been up to!" Or possibly not. Maybe the Lord told David one breezy afternoon day as David was leading his sheep to green pastures about his giant-killing destiny. The point isn't whether he did or didn't know -- God will do both. The point is that David was intentional to do things when he was hidden that allowed him to experience the blessing and favor of the Lord in many seasons.

Jesus loves you so much, He won't allow your destiny to kill you or His blessings to crumble you! That's why we have a choice to lean into humility and hiddenness. I love my kids and because of my love, I will not give my ten-year-old my car keys or my fifteen-year-old access to her college fund. Those are blessings that I have saved for them to enjoy once they have built the maturity and wisdom to use those blessings well. Until they can, what I have for them isn't a blessing -- it is a curse!

The goal of scripture is to connect us with God by teaching us about Him and His heart. The more time we spend with Jesus, the more emotionally mature we become. This is what transformation is (**2 Corinthians 2:18**). Every mature person who can handle the blessings of the Lord goes through at least one season of obscurity. Being hidden is for our benefit. The goal is to value obscurity for what it produces while not running in front of the Lord to get out prematurely. His word says in **Matthew 23:12 (NIV)**, "Whoever exalts himself will be humbled, and whoever humbles himself will be exalted."

Obscurity is the place where maturity and wisdom become a part of our character.

EVEN SO TODAY, THOUGH IT MEANS BEING DESPISED AND MISUNDERSTOOD, GET ALONE IN THE WILDERNESS OF QUIET AND STILLNESS BEFORE GOD. SEEK HIS FACE TILL YOUR SOUL IS KINDLED WITH THE FLAMES OF LOVE FROM THE BURNING BUSH.

Aimee Semple McPherson

8

IDENTIFYING OUR ASSIGNMENT

I HAVE FOUND WHAT I BELIEVE TO BE THE HIGHEST KIND OF CHRISTIANITY. I WANT TO GIVE MY LIFE, GOD HELPING ME, TO LEAD OTHERS, MANY OTHERS, TO FIND IT. MANY HAVE FOUND IT ALREADY, THANK GOD, AND THEY ARE DOING WHAT I AM DOING, IN A LARGE OR LITTLE WAY, AS GOD GIVES THEM LIGHT. AND THAT IS ALL THERE IS TO THE REVIVAL, AND THERE IS TO ME MY FRIEND.
Evan Roberts

REVIVALISTS ARE THERMOSTATS, not thermometers. They set the spiritual temperature rather than reflecting it. They rise above their mood or confidence and set a new standard. They understand that going to higher levels requires swimming upstream against the flow of fear, self-doubt, past failures, people's opinions, insecurities, and lies. They overcome reflecting the status quo and believe they are anointed to bring Kingdom impact and change, no matter how they feel.

The enemy hopes we will limit our assignment or ministry to times when we feel anointed, bold, empowered, or prepared. Revivalists know that we have an anointing that abides. The anointing of God flows from the Holy Spirit inside of us **(1 John 2:20)**. It's simple really: you have a Holy influencer inside of you and He needs to get out! This is one of the ways we make Earth like Heaven -- by filling it with the Spirit of God.

When I was a senior in high school, I had to decide which college I should attend. I had scholarships for my voice from multiple schools. I made an old fashioned pros and cons list, assessed the financial cost of each school, and how much debt I would be in once I had finished. I felt as if the weight of the world was on my shoulders in this decision. Maybe you have been in a similar situation. I came to my mom crying because deep in my heart, more than guided by a cost-benefit analysis, I wanted to be in the will of God.

My mom told me something so powerful that unlocked my ability to choose. She said, "Christina, God's will is not a bullseye. You don't have to stress about hitting it in the middle with one shot. God wants you in His will more than you do. Your heart is good, and if you make a choice wanting to honor Him He will make it work out for you! You are in His will because of how you are pursuing Him. He gave you options because He wants you to make a choice."

As soon as she said that, I knew instantly which college I wanted to go to. My desire of wanting so badly to be in God's will wasn't bad but it was misdirected energy. It limited my ability to feel free in His love and limited my identity as His kiddo. It took the fun out of the opportunity. Without the pressure of having to hit the bullseye, I was able to make a good choice and enter into a new assignment from the Lord. Too many people struggle similarly. We encounter the Lord, receive His love, commissions, authority, and power, and then wonder, "What is His will for my life?" This wondering can paralyze us if we do not recognize that God gives us the ability to choose much of our destiny.

He made it simple. He said to heal the sick, raise the dead, cleanse the lepers, drive out demons, and give away what He gave us (Matthew 10:8). The bullseye isn't a profession, a career, or the answer to what we want to be when we grow up. We can choose what we want to spend our time on and His will is that we bring healing, resurrection (revival), wholeness, freedom, and anything else He has given us along the way. It's as if He says, "Do what makes you come alive and bring Me with you!"

For heaven to be released around us, we will naturally spend time praying for others, sharing Christ, declaring healings and miracles, teaching and prophesying. It is equally as important to acknowledge that the same anointing empowers us to do family life well, steward our finances, manage our sex drives, and have a thriving marriage. Those living in Christ are carriers of an anointing that is contagious. The world becomes attracted to it because we have the answers they are looking for. It's less about what we are born to do and more about who we were born to love. Less about where our skills take us more about where love takes us.

It comes down to what we believe because what we believe has power over our lives. If you believe you are powerful in the Lord, you will be powerful. If you believe you are a revivalist, revival fires will be sparked around you. If you believe you are anointed, you will impact the world for Christ.

For many years, I had the opportunity to be a part of the Healing Room team in our city. A man that I had never met came in to get prayer for his knee and an upcoming surgery that he had scheduled. As we were praying for his knee, I had a prophetic word for him. I told him, "You were born to run. I don't just mean naturally, but also in your assignment from Jesus, your purpose. Other people around you are telling you to slow down and pace yourself but the Lord made you with the ability to run faster than others. You have a high capacity and are able to do many things at once."

He started crying and almost fell into my arms. When he composed himself from the tears and shock, he told me, "I am a missionary in Belize. I have so many dreams and things in my heart that I want to do. Every time I bring it up to the people I am accountable to they shoot me down, tell me I need to go slow, and not take on too much. It has made me so confused because I hear God telling me something different."

We celebrated the word of the Lord that brought Him freedom and prayed again for those dreams to be birthed and for his healing, so he didn't have to spend time in recovery. Later I found out that he was healed and didn't need surgery after all! It was a miracle from God! But it was also a prophetic sign to this man that those words -- that he was born to run in his life and calling -- were true. So much so that he didn't need surgery! He could do the things God had assigned him. The council he had been given was wise, but it wasn't right for him. God had given him an assignment for Belize, and he needed the freedom to run after it.

GOD IS FAMOUS FOR ACCOMPLISHING EXTRAORDINARY THINGS WITH ORDINARY PEOPLE.
Kris Vallotton

Your assignment is not your job description, career, or role. It is more than a task and might not be included on your resume. It is where the grace of God or anointing is in your life. It may be the same your whole life, it may look different at times or in seasons, but it will always be empowered by your gift and your desire to follow -- to be in the same way with -- Jesus.

It is very important that we can identify what our assignments are in each season of our lives. Once we know what they are, we can protect them.

About a year ago I was talking to the Lord and He said, "I want you to be vigilant in your assignment." I don't use that word often so I looked it up. Vigilant means 'to be watchful and alert, especially to avoid danger'. At the time, my assignment was to bring structure, change, and reformation to our church staff. My job description said "Children's Pastor", but my assignment was to instigate reformation and build new structures. I did both of those things while doing the will of God - praying for the sick, bringing freedom to the captives, and making my home a place where Jesus dwells. See how that all works together? Honestly though, at the time, my assignment was cloudy. It knew I was asking the right questions, but the answers led to some pain and frustration. I was discouraged. The Lord brought me to look at Jesus' life to teach me how to be vigilant over my assignment.

And before He had finished speaking, people arrived from Jairus' house and pushed through the crowd to give Jairus the news: "There's no need to trouble the master any longer—your daughter has died." But Jesus refused to listen to what they were told and said to the Jewish official, "Don't yield to fear. All you need to do is to keep on believing." So they left for his home, but Jesus didn't allow anyone to go with them except Peter and the two brothers, Jacob and John.

When they arrived at the home of the synagogue ruler, they encountered a noisy uproar among the people, for they were all weeping and wailing. Upon entering the home, Jesus said to them, "Why all this grief and weeping? Don't you know the girl is not dead but merely asleep?" Then everyone began to ridicule and make fun of him. But He threw them all outside.

Then He took the child's father and mother and his three disciples and went into the room where the girl was lying. He tenderly clasped the child's hand in his and said to her in Aramaic, "Talitha koum," which means, "Little girl, wake up from the sleep of death." Instantly the twelve-year-old girl sat up, stood to her feet, and started walking around the room! Everyone was overcome with astonishment in seeing this miracle! **Mark 5:35-42 (TPT)**

Jesus left a crowd of people who wanted something from Him to visit a dead girl that did not ask for Him. We can learn something right here that is so valuable. Jesus wasn't moved by a schedule, facts, or needs. He was connected to the voice of God, which informed His decisions. God receives the greatest return on His investment in us when we are connected to His voice. Jesus was led by God, not led by what was good.

We can also see that Jesus went out on assignment to heal Jairus' daughter, but the people around Him didn't know what His assignment was. He knew that their opinions didn't matter, but we're still powerful! So to protect or be vigilant in His assignment, He told those mocking and ridiculing the power of God to leave! Jesus refused to reduce His assignment to what people thought or said...

He kicked them out and silenced their influence.

By being vigilant He was intentional, "But Jesus refused to listen to what they were told and said to the Jewish official, "Don't yield to fear. All you need to do is to keep on believing." **(Mark 5:36)** Jesus was possessed by God's promises rather than man's. He sought to please His Father in heaven not His peers on Earth. We see this throughout His life in how His disciples questioned Him and how He taught them. As I read through the gospels, it is as if He knew something they didn't know (wink wink). This eventually led to Him choosing the cross which shows me Jesus also was not a victim to His assignment. He chose it and focused on you and me, the joy before Him **(Hebrews 12:2)** so he could finish His assignment well. Your assignment is heaven's investment in you for this season. How are you being vigilant over it?

I like how Bill Johnson encourages believers in this. He says, "When you discover your assignment, you have a responsibility in prayer to pursue the gifts that validate your assignment. Too many people define their ministry by what they are good at. You define your ministry by what God said and then get alone with Him and cry out to Him for the anointing that validates who He said you are." It may be easy for us to confuse our identity and our ministry. Our assignment and our anointings. Our role in the Kingdom and our opportunity in our families. We can not be vigilant if we cannot separate who we are from what we do and who we are becoming, and we can not burn forever unless we have clarity over the two.

FAITH DOES NOT OPERATE IN THE REALM OF THE POSSIBLE.
THERE IS NO GLORY FOR GOD IN THAT WHICH IS HUMANLY
POSSIBLE. FAITH BEGINS WHERE MAN'S POWER ENDS.
George Müller

EVAN ROBERTS IS one of my favorite revivalists. He was 26 years old when revival broke in Wales. His story is very similar to some of ours: he grew up in a Christian home, then went to work in an ordinary profession as a laborer in a coal mine. In his free time, he would study the Bible and pray. The more time he spent with God the more and more passionate he became; he believed he had been given an assignment from God to minister God's love to others, so he enrolled in a college to study theology. Just two weeks after arriving at the school, Roberts took part in a convention (similar to what we would call a conference) where he had a life-changing encounter with God which he described as "A fresh baptism of the spirit." This marked his life significantly. He wrote about this time and said,

One Friday night last spring, when praying by my bedside before retiring, I was taken up to a great expanse – without time and space. It was communion with God. Before this, I had a far-off God. I was frightened that night but never since. So great was my shivering that I rocked the bed, and my brother, being awakened, took hold of me, thinking I was ill. After that experience, I was awakened every night, a little after one o'clock. This was most strange, for through the years I slept like a rock, and no disturbance in my room would awaken me. From that hour I was taken up into the divine fellowship for about four hours. What it was I cannot tell you, except that it was divine. About five o'clock I was again allowed to sleep on till about nine. At this time I was again taken up into the same experience as in the earlier hours of the morning until about twelve or one o'clock. . . . This went on for three months.[15]

Soon after, on 29 September 1904, at a small church, he preached a message about repentance from sin and encouraged the listeners to get rid of any doubts they might have about the significance of God in their lives, to obey the Holy Spirit and to confess publicly that they would follow Christ. By the end of the week, sixty people had repented from their sins and Roberts went on to host revivalist meetings in each of the mining towns. Not one dollar was spent promoting the revival or Roberts. Within a year over 100,000 people had received Christ and joined the church.

He was particularly influential to those who were young and in need of direction for their lives. It was said he, "Gave them fire in their bellies and hope in their hearts." The effects of the anointing on his life didn't just stop with salvations; crime rates dropped wherever he came to preach and huge numbers of people gave up alcohol. Soon pubs were closing in England as cities held revivalist meetings. I have heard it said the people who traveled by boat from England to Wales would feel the difference in the atmosphere the second they would get off the boat. Others said it felt like a spirit of conviction was in the air, others said it felt like heaven in Wales.

By 1906 Roberts fell ill. He had, almost literally, worked himself into the ground and suffered both a physical and emotional breakdown. He removed himself from the public to heal and gave himself for the years following to prayer and intercession. He also spent some time writing. Many people were disappointed after his recovery that he didn't go back to preaching and holding meetings, but he believed that he reached more people for salvation and healing through private prayer then public teaching.

PRAYER IS MORE IMPORTANT TO ME THAN FOOD.
Evan Roberts

Though there is some controversy (there always will be when we are living for Jesus) about the influences and decisions he made in the later years of his life, Roberts' life models for us exactly what it means to identify the assignment given to us for a season, pair it with the anointing (grace) of God and the favor of God on our lives, and then be used by God to give away what we have received -- be a living flame of His love. I wonder if your thoughts have been challenged about your assignment as you have read through this chapter? Or maybe you find yourself feeling known.

I remember the first message I listened to by Kris Vallotton when he was encouraging people at Bethel Church to be tipping points. He said multiple times, "You were born to be amazing. You were born to make a difference!" I remember feeling something unlock within me. I felt as though I could breathe for the first time and that the deepest parts of my heart was known. I needed someone else to acknowledge that I had a divine destiny that was great and if I could accomplish the dreams in my heart without the grace of God then I was dreaming too small. That message was used by God to change so much in me -- it built my resolve and grit to run and never look back!

Living for Jesus is hard. Compromise is always an option. Quitting is tempting. But you and I were born to do hard things. We aren't superheroes but we are supernatural, and fatigue is real. Throughout the years I have turned to **Hebrews 12** when I become tired, disillusioned, or frustrated with my assignment. Within moments of reading it and being face-to-face with Jesus -- who embraced His assignment and "plowed through" for me -- I become revitalized again, revived again, and motivated by love again to burn!

Do you see what this means—all these pioneers who blazed the way, all these veterans cheering us on? It means we'd better get on with it. Strip down, start running—and never quit! No extra spiritual fat, no parasitic sins. Keep your eyes on Jesus, who both began and finished this race we're in. Study how He did it. Because He never lost sight of where He was headed—that exhilarating finish in and with God—He could put up with anything along the way: Cross, shame, whatever. And now He's there, in the place of honor, right alongside God. When you find yourselves flagging in your faith, go over that story again, item by item, that long litany of hostility He plowed through. That will shoot adrenaline into your souls! **Hebrews 12:1-3 (MSG)**

IT IS NO SMALL COMFORT TO ME TO KNOW THAT GOD HAS CALLED ME TO MY WORK, PUTTING ME WHERE I AM AND AS I AM. I HAVE NOT SOUGHT THE POSITION, AND I DARE NOT LEAVE IT. HE KNOWS WHY HE PLACES ME HERE -- WHETHER TO DO, TO LEARN, OR SUFFER.
J. Hudson Taylor

9

NATURALLY SUPERNATURAL

MEN HAVE MYSTIFIED AND PHILOSOPHIZED THE GOSPEL OF
JESUS BUT IT IS AS SIMPLE AS IT CAN BE. THE SECRET OF
CHRISTIANITY IS IN BEING. IT IS IN BEING A POSSESSOR OF
THE NATURE OF JESUS CHRIST.
John G. Lake

LET'S get back to scripture!

As Jesus left the house, two blind men began following Him, shouting
out over and over, "Son of David, show us mercy and heal us!" And
they followed Him right into the house where Jesus was staying. So
Jesus asked them, "Do you believe that I have the power to restore
sight to your eyes?"

They replied, "Yes Lord, we believe!"

Then Jesus put His hands over their eyes and said, "You will have
what your faith expects!" And instantly their eyes opened—they
could see! Then Jesus warned them sternly, "Make sure that you tell

no one what just happened!" But unable to contain themselves, they went out and spread the news everywhere! **Matthew 9: 27-30 (TPT)**

Let's be real, I couldn't keep quiet either! I've needed corrective lenses since the third grade. I don't exactly know what it's like to be blind, but I'm close! Even my kids know not to ask me to look at anything in the morning until I put my eyes in! But that phrase that Jesus says -- "You will have what your faith expects" -- gets me! Did Jesus say this because they believed He was able to do miracles? Or was it because when they called out "Son of David" they proved they believed in who He was? Other than the wise men, these two blind men were the first to recognize Jesus as King even without their vision.[16] There is something so powerful in recognizing who He is and that in Him lies all power and ability to heal.

They were healed, instantly. Jesus didn't pray, Jesus did not cast out a demon of blindness, He did not lead them through inner healing or break off generational curses. He touched them and they could see. Imagine His eyes and tender look of love being the first thing they were able to see! We seek to follow His example! I bet Jesus always had a smile on His face when He healed His kids. I imagine the great delight He must have experienced every time He touched someone in desperate need and they recognized what they really needed was His touch and His eyes meeting theirs.

I recall in my teenage years my mom would pray for me and my sisters with this phrase, "Lord as they go about their day, let them be naturally supernatural." Because I was a teenage punk, I wasn't sure what she was praying, nor did I show that I cared much. I am sure we talked about it and she tried to explain, (parents your kids may not listen at the moment, but rest assured, you're bringing life) but I didn't think much of it. Now, I pray it over myself, my staff, my kids, my leaders, because it is awesome! She was declaring over us that I would go about my day and release the impossible, the incomprehensible, the unpopular but deeply desirable reality that heaven would invade Earth by our normal comings and goings. She was prophesying an effortless lifestyle in my ability to do what Jesus did.

She was also instilling in me the ease that comes from being anointed and connected to the Spirit of God with the language of naturally supernatural. I believe this reflects God's heart for us! We are not separated from supernatural activity until we earn it. It is a part of us... naturally!

A REVIVALIST LIFESTYLE is empowered through our identity as sons and daughters of God. Understanding that Jesus paid a high price to give us -- His followers -- His identity. Living as His friends is the best way we can honor Him. It's in Him that we become the best version of ourselves. As we see Him we become like Him. Through encounter with Jesus we get saved, healed, freed, and a transfer of identity takes place. As the Bible says, we become a new creation (**2 Corinthians 5:17**). We become prone to righteousness, prone to love; His very nature changes us so we can change the world around us. We are called to reign in life as sons and daughters of God. Everything we do should be out of that position and perspective. Influencing the world around us with the attributes of heaven then becomes an outflow of who we've been changed into, and the outflow of how His love has affected us... naturally supernatural.

Once I connected to this truth, I put a demand on Heaven. I had read so much, listened to so many podcasts, and sat in so many services. I remember talking to the Lord while I was doing the dishes and sayings, "You said I can do greater things than You did on Earth. Prove it." I wasn't being smart or irreverent. I was hungry! If it was true and if I was willing to risk and put myself out there then I was asking Him to show up! Honestly, I don't think He was offended. At least He has never told me He was. I think He felt invited to show off in my life! But He didn't show off right away. I prayed for sick people who didn't get healed, I took more classes, learned different theories and practices, prayed with more faith and saw migraines healed, legs grew out, peace came over people, but nothing greater than what Jesus did.

I could have quit or kept going. I kept going. I prayed for deep healing for people who had massive trauma, I started prophesying jobs, healing, and destinies over people. As a result of my and other people's prayers, I saw PTSD, sexual trauma, heavy sexual addiction, generational curses, all bow to the name of Jesus! I have testimonies of people who had struggled to get jobs, struggle to get whole, struggle to hear God's voice, supernaturally touched and changed in a moment.

Still, from my current seat, the only greater things I have done than Jesus are being married for fourteen years, raising three kids, and being in ministry longer than three years! (I just laughed and threw up at the same time). For real though, don't take that away from me!

I am grateful for every healing I have been able to be a part of! It has been an honor to see what love has done in so many people's lives through my yes. And I am relentlessly and unapologetically longing for more! Years ago, I listened to a message when Todd White (look into this guy!) verified that he had prayed for healing for one thousand people before he saw one person healed. When I heard this I cried, I felt encouraged and sorry for the dude! Shoot, I keep track of a lot of testimonies and stories but can't say I've calculated how many people I have prayed for! Those of you who know him, know I shouldn't feel sorry for him at all! He is one who lives as a revivalist and has testimony after testimony of miracles, signs, and wonders that he has been a part of.

I dream about seeing someone I pray for who has cancer healed. I want to see someone get out of a wheelchair, and a couple reconciled in the marriage they thought was dead. I remember the first time I prayed for someone who couldn't hear. When her ears opened up I was just as shocked as she was! We both cried. I was so grateful to the Lord and so in awe of His great love for her! All I wanted to do was protect her from becoming a spectacle in the middle of the church service. I could imagine that after years of not hearing she was having a profound encounter with Love Himself in that moment. The next time I prayed over a man's ears they didn't open. I was heartbroken! I had even more faith this time but for whatever reason, he wasn't healed.

Throughout scripture, we see that Jesus heals in multiple ways. Even when He was on Earth He didn't model a formula or specific way to acquire results. But we do see that every person who came to Him was healed (Luke 6:19), which tells me this is the standard! I cannot explain why I've seen healing sometimes and why at other times I've haven't. I can't theologically explain what works at times and what doesn't.

For a while after reading **Matthew 18:18** I tried binding sickness and loosening health. Sometimes it worked. I remember binding my six-year-old's ear infection and the pain leaving in five minutes (that's how you know it was Jesus and not the Motrin! LOL). But there were other times it didn't work. I've commanded healing, prayed in the name of Jesus Christ of Nazareth instead of just Jesus, and prayed to Jehovah Rapha to prove to the demonic powers of sickness and disease my Biblical knowledge.

AT THE BEGINNING of my journey as a living flame of love, I had the opportunity to go on a ministry trip to a church in Oregon. I remember our first night we held a healing service. This was going to be my opportunity to be a part of the action. My first time seeing a major miracle. My first time on stage releasing a word of knowledge for healing. I didn't hear a word from God for anyone, so I borrowed one of my sister's words and pretended it was mine. Revivalists don't wait till they have it all figured out -- we've surrendered the preference of comfort -- we throw caution to the wind and embrace risk hidden inside the learning journey!

When we were done with our time ministering on the platform, I went over to pray for a woman. I asked her name, and I still remember how delicately she responded with, "Rose." She was frail, tired-looking, and young. I asked her what I could pray for and she replied she had MS, an autoimmune disorder, and another serious illness I didn't know how to pronounce.

I was ready to see Rose healed. I prayed from a place of great faith. I commanded things to go. I released healing and then checked in with her to see how she was feeling. Nothing had changed. I saw people all around me experiencing breakthroughs. I tried again and invited the Holy Spirit. I commanded the pain to leave, and for her body to be restored...

Nothing happened!

I was tempted in my mind to hug her, bless her, and move on so I could go and be a part of wherever the action was. But I choose to stay with her and try again. After a few attempts, when I couldn't think of anything else to pray over her or say, she laid down in my lap, and I stroked her hair for the rest of the service.

God didn't heal her that night. I didn't witness any healings. Lots of other people went on stage and shared testimonies and I didn't see a single miracle. I was bummed, discouraged, and confused. The next day when we returned for the next service Rose found me. She hugged me and told me that every other time she had asked for prayer, people would pray for her and move on. She noticed people avoided her or tried to avoid making eye contact with her. No one had ever spent more than a polite five minutes with her – let alone an hour. She said the love of Jesus she felt overpowered the feelings of pain in her body. She experienced the love of Jesus that day because I chose to be with her.

I was stunned. Her response made all the disappointment and confusion go away. I was so focused on the miracles, I forgot that the greatest gift is love. To receive the mandate that night to spend time releasing the heart of the King through love was an honor. I love being a part of the family business! Even though I didn't really know what I was doing, I am so grateful I didn't sacrifice love for a different story.

I have shared this experience with others in large and small groups and the funny thing is, every time I share it people receive healing from rejection, isolation, insecurity, and physical pain. The last time I shared it and prayed for a woman who had massive back pain for ten years as a result of an injury from a car accident. She was instantly touched by love and was reduced in her pain level from an intense ten (which she said was normal) to a three. I gave her my number and checked in with her the next day. She slept the entire night through for the first time in longer than she could remember and testified that it was as if love was blanketed around her all night long. Her pain was still significantly reduced, she was rested, at peace, and in gratitude over how the Lord had touched her body, soul, and spirit. Learning to love hasn't changed my theology on the finished work of Jesus -- it continually reveals more about it!

What I learned with every miracle, every wonder, every healing, is that God is good. He loves and wills to heal us even more than I want people to be healed. I have a choice to get frustrated with what I am not seeing or to trust that Jesus is touching His kids no matter what I see. I can allow the lack of results to keep me from praying -- which I have done at times -- or I can push through the questions and discomfort into my destiny of being naturally supernatural! Some days, I am guilty of getting frustrated, of becoming discouraged, of having a lack of faith that God will even use me. This is a place where I have had to battle against the lies in my mind that would disqualify me from living a life of a revivalist where supernatural activity flows out of who I am.

Maybe you have heard the lies and doubts too? "If you would stop yelling at your kids, God will actually use you." Or, "What right do I have to pray for that person when I haven't read my Bible in a week?" Or the best one, "Does God really want all His kids healed?" Once the lie is exposed it sounds silly, yet so many people I know have been stuck in the middle of one. Revivalists aren't perfect or immune to doubt. Revivalists overcome doubt and choose to enter into a lifestyle of having what our faith expects.

When you pray, there is no need to repeat empty phrases, praying like those who don't know God, for they expect God to hear them because of their many words. There is no need to imitate them, since your Father already knows what you need before you ask Him. Pray like this:

'Our Father, dwelling in the heavenly realms,
may the glory of your name
be the center on which our lives turn.
Manifest your kingdom realm,
and cause your every purpose to be fulfilled
on Earth, just as it is fulfilled in heaven.'
Matthew 6:7-10 TPT

If we were in a classroom environment together, I would have you highlight and repeat verse 10. Say it with me if you'd like -- manifest your kingdom realm and cause your every purpose to be fulfilled on Earth. Jesus is once again revealing the intention and will of God through the Lord's prayer: for God to manifest His kingdom realm. Jesus is asking, "Dad, would You display Your nature on Earth!" He is teaching us that not only is it God's will, but that it is possible!

AFTER EVERYTHING we've learned on our journey about the Lord making Himself vulnerable to us by partnering with us, showing us His will to heal the sick, raise the dead and so on, all while allowing us to live a life of evidence of His existence and love -- how then do we experience Earth like heaven?

Great question! I believe it's in the cultivation of our environments!

In order for the Lord to manifest His kingdom realm -- which simply means 'display His nature' -- we need to create an environment for Him to inhabit. We do that in us and around us! Similarly to a gardener who tends to the land, believers in Jesus Christ are invited to prepare the soil to host the seed which holds the promise of the fruit of heaven.

'Cultivate' is a verb that means 'develop land for growing'. To cultivate the culture of the kingdom of God in your home, workplace, church campus, or park means to develop your heart to grow the values of Jesus. It's included in all we've been talking about -- love, fire, passion, surrender, and encounter. But it's also so much more! It involves devotion, activation, risk, and faithfulness, and much more. It is found in many seasons of harvesting, sowing, and reaping which results in spending an entire lifetime of being 'in the same way with' Jesus and transformed into the image of Christ **(2 Corinthians 3:18)**. It happens naturally and supernaturally and attracts the attention of heaven as well as the people around us.

LIVING WITH FAITH AND COURAGE IS SOMETHING THAT LIFE REQUIRES OF EACH OF US. NEVER, ABSOLUTELY NEVER, GIVE UP! NEVER GIVE IN NO MATTER WHAT! FIGHT IT THROUGH! AND I PROMISE YOU SOMETHING WITH ALL OF MY HEART -- GOD WILL HELP YOU.
Kathryn Kuhlman

10

CULTURAL IMPLICATIONS

ALL GOD'S GIANTS HAVE BEEN WEAK MEN WHO DID GREAT THINGS FOR GOD BECAUSE THEY RECKONED ON GOD BEING WITH THEM.
J. Hudson Taylor

FOR HIS SECOND-GRADE biography book report, Ethan, my second child, picked Jackie Robinson. I don't know why -- he refuses to play baseball and is more entertained with video games and Legos. Being a softball player myself I didn't question him. I hopped right on board and joined in the conversation. "Do you know he was--"

"The first black Major League baseball player," he finished my sentence. He always loves to one-up me and prove he is smarter than I am (It doesn't take much!). We discussed his ball-playing career at UCLA and his infamous number that was retired. It was well into the conversation when he asked me if I knew who Rickey was? Trying to connect the dots and realizing I had no idea who Rickey was I shook my head no.

"Rickey is the world changer," he said confidently.

"Rickey? Do you mean Jackie because he was the ballplayer?"

"No mom, Rickey is the one who gave Jackie the chance to play baseball. He is the world-changer of the story."

I gasped as I realized the weightiness of the moment. Jackie changed baseball but Branch Rickey changed the world. I've been telling my kids every day before they hop out of the car for school that they are world changers. They change the world multiple times a day when they smile, when they sit next to a lonely kid, when they encourage a student, when they stand up to a bully, when they pick up trash. Every moment is an opportunity to make a difference in the world and impact those around us. I've taught them that changing the world happens in the culmination of hundreds of little moments and to stay faithful to release the kingdom of God as they go about their normal, mundane, everyday life.

Ethan has this revelation so deep in him that he was able to identify it in someone else's life and legacy. I wonder if Rickey intended to change the world when he gave Jackie Robinson an invitation to change baseball. He did intend to change something! He chose to lock eyes with a broken culture and bring Heaven's justice into a broken system. This was a huge risk for him individually and professionally. When asked about this decision, Rickey commented that he simply, "Thought it was God's work."

A LIFE IS NOT IMPORTANT EXCEPT IN THE
IMPACT IT HAS ON OTHERS LIVES.
Jackie Robinson

AS REVIVALISTS, we have a responsibility to transfer the kingdom of heaven from our hearts to our homes and then to the world around us. As I have studied revivalists in the church and outside of the church, I haven't read anyone say, "I woke up one morning and thought to myself, today I am going to impact culture and change the world by this monumental act." From what I've researched they made a decision in their heart to burn for the Lord, take a risk, engage with the world around them and allow whatever came their way to come. Changing the world might not feel or look monumental as it is happening. We may not even be able to identify it as, "THIS IS A WORLD-CHANGING MOMENT." Nevertheless, moments like that are all around us. You are changing the world as you:

- Parent your kids
- Stop to give dignity to a person on the street in need
- Apply yourself to a degree program that is a part of your dream
- Study scriptures to find out about the nature of God and His Kingdom
- Pray for your family
- Take risks to share what God is saying about the person in front of you at the store

You are an agent of transformation. You change the world as you smile while you are waiting in line at the grocery store. You are called to be a world-changer and make a cultural impact around you! You, me, and every believer has a role to play in the fulfillment of Revelations 11:15 (NIV) which says, "The seventh angel sounded his trumpet, and there were loud voices in heaven, which said: 'The kingdom of the world has become the kingdom of our Lord and of his Messiah, and He will reign forever and ever.'" This is what it looks like to implicate the culture of heaven, which is inside of us around us. The kingdoms of the world become the kingdom of our Lord. Another way to say that is that the world's system comes under the authority of heaven's system.

Revival changes culture. It is that simple. And changing or influencing culture isn't a temporary assignment -- it's your destiny.

IF YOU READ HISTORY, YOU WILL FIND THAT THE CHRISTIANS WHO DID MOST FOR THE PRESENT WORLD WERE PRECISELY THOSE WHO THOUGHT MOST OF THE NEXT. IT IS SINCE CHRISTIANS HAVE LARGELY CEASED TO THINK OF THE OTHER WORLD THAT THEY HAVE BECOME SO INEFFECTIVE IN THIS ONE.
C.S. Lewis

DURING WORLD WAR II, on February 15th, 1942 the British surrendered and 60,000 soldiers were captured in Japan. Ernest Gordon, a Scottish battalion soldier was among these 60,000, but he was able to briefly escape his Japanese captors and attempted to make his way to Indonesia. However, he was captured by the Imperial Japanese Navy warship who transported him and others back to Singapore.

Along with hundreds of other prisoners, Gordon was force marched from Singapore to the Jungles of Siam, where they would all participate in the construction of the Death Railway and the Bridge on the River Kwai. He was to be imprisoned in what they called a death camp. In this camp, it was the intent of the Japanese soldiers to crush

the spirits of the prisoners of war (POW) and take away their humanity by whatever means necessary which included punishment, torture, and humiliation.

During his years as a POW, he suffered the effects of numerous illnesses and diseases including malnutrition, malaria, diphtheria, typhoid, jungle ulcers, various parasites, and an operation to remove a kidney, performed without pain relief. Gordon was so close to death that the Japanese soldiers placed him in a separate barrack called the "Death Ward", an area specifically set aside for prisoners who were dying. Even though there was no hope of survival for Gordon, some friends built a small shelter for him, and two men in particular came to his aid. One was Dusty Miller, a Protestant Christian who was a gardener in civilian life, and Dinty Moore, a Roman Catholic man who alternated shifts bathing Gordon, caring for his wounds, and massaging his legs to help him gain the strength to walk again.

With these acts of kindness, Gordon experienced the love and grace of Jesus Christ and his interest in religion grew. Previously, religion in the camps had been transactional: prisoners turned to God for relief, and, when that relief did not appear in short order, they were no longer interested. For Gordon, it was everything but transactional. He regained his strength and made a full recovery, soon leaving the Death Ward and joining the rest of the prisoners in the camp.

He was witness to two more particular acts of selfless compassion (unknown world-changing moments) that changed his life forever, as well as the camp. One prisoner was discovered to have starved himself to death to provide rations for a dying friend. The other was a story I will never forget.

One day as the prisoners were coming back from their labor on the railroad, the work party lost a shovel. Upon return to the death camp, a Japanese guard threatened the entire party with execution unless the guilty prisoner came forward. One POW stepped forward and said it was him. He was beaten to death by the guard in front of the rest of the men as a statement to maintain the environment of fear and servitude. Shortly after it was discovered that the guard had miscounted the inventory, and the missing shovel had been there all along.

These acts of magnificent self-giving as well as his own relationship with Jesus Christ sparked hope and revival of souls inside the prison walls! Gordon started teaching and sharing the love of God and referencing the kindness of Miller and Moore as they were living like true disciples of Jesus Christ. The prisoners soon regained their fundamental human qualities. A sense of wonder about truth, beauty, and goodness in a place utterly deprived of all three was restored. They became men again; transformed back into their original designs from God instead of the inhumane, selfish, and distraught beasts they had become. This started to breed hunger and a desire to learn and grow within the camp.

Gordon set up a university for the men in order to continue driving them and add purpose and direction to their lives. Initially, it was carried out in secret; eventually, the Japanese guards allowed it. A theatre was established, a ballet was performed, and books were supernaturally discovered that led to classes being taught at night. An orchestra came together using instruments from a Red Cross shipment that the Japanese had no use for, as well as woodwinds crafted from bamboo trees. Also, a church was established, which held Christian services.

From these small moments of risk and love, physical kindness, and compassion, a culture emerged. Civilization returned to the minds and hearts of men, and along with it came faith. Here is Gordon's description of the crucial intervention of grace: "The wind of the spirit had blown upon us; we could not prove how or whence it had come. But our experience pointed to a source beyond ourselves. We knew personal fulfillment, love, joy, peace, wholeness, as we committed ourselves to the one who called us. Only as we responded to this Word did we receive the power to progress towards true humanity. Our life on the horizontal plane was made meaningful at the point where it was met by the vertical. At the point marked by the Cross, we found ourselves."

While Moore and Miller were never freed from the camp, Gordon survived, went back to Scotland to become an ordained minister preaching forgiveness and repentance in Jesus Christ! He was greatly used by God to change the culture of a death camp into a city of God where life, love, beauty, and creativity bloomed.

THERE ARE many revivalists who ran into dark places like Amy Charmicheal, Heidi Baker, and David Livingston. There are some who were imprisoned for what they believe like Richard Wurmbrand, Dietrich Bonhoeffer, and Corrie Ten Boom. Others who left their homes and families to pursue their assignments: Hudson Taylor, Jim and Elizabeth Elliot, and Helen Roseveare. Modern-day revivalists who are pursuing their assignments through their areas of influence including Russel Wilson, Kanye, and Akiane. There are others that will never be written down in books or blogs, yet carry the same significance and have impacted culture.

There are testimonies and stories, like the one I am about to share, (from an acquaintance I met years ago) about some details from a mission trip. One normal random day, Jostein, a young man from Norway, traveled to a dump in a nameless city in a small country in South America.

Days earlier, this young man was full of vigor, hope, and love. With a heart filled with love and compassion he intentionally embraced the forgotten and unlovable in a dump. Set in the outskirts of the city, this dump was known for its sleaziness, drug use, and extreme poverty. However, that didn't stop Jostein or his team. It made the opportunity to see how far love would take him even more alluring. There wasn't a plan, a program, or an audience but his heart was arrested as he turned to see a grown man in his mid-forties stumbling across the top of the trash dump completely strung out and naked.

That's right, butt-naked except for the pants that hung at his ankles barely held up by a single worn-out shoe. His entire dirty emaciated body was exposed for all to see. At first sight, Jostein's heart melted with great compassion, and he didn't skip a beat as he started pursuing the man while bending down to pick up trash. Everyone around couldn't help but stare, wondering (as we all are) what his next step was.

Jostein bent down before the naked man and started pulling his pants up over his calves, his knees, and his waist. He then took the trash he had been collecting and started to fasten suspenders. In a brief moment, dignity and honor had been restored to this man as the shame of his nakedness and sin was covered. But love didn't stop there.

Jostein took the leftover trash that he had collected and made himself a hat and a belt. Soon everyone in the dump had different clothing items made out of smelly trash that they were joyfully wearing. The night continued with dancing, dinner, and great fun. For this one night, they all forgot their inhospitable location and that their personal accessories were pieces of discarded garbage no one valued or wanted to be around. Everyone had equal value, and everyone was given an opportunity to meet Love Himself and many did. The kingdom of God is righteousness, peace, and joy in the Holy Spirit **(Romans 14:17)**, and the kingdom was expressed beautifully in that place.

THE MOST IMPORTANT THING IS THAT WE ARE ABLE TO BE ONE-ON-ONE, YOU AND I WITH EACH OTHER AT THE MOMENT. IF WE CAN BE PRESENT TO THE MOMENT WITH THE PERSON THAT WE HAPPEN TO BE WITH, THAT'S WHAT'S IMPORTANT.
Fred Rogers

THE INSTIGATED BY LOVE

THE ONLY REASON WE DO NOT HAVE REVIVAL IS BECAUSE WE ARE WILLING TO LIVE WITHOUT IT.
Leonard Ravenhill

IN **GENESIS CHAPTER 1 and 2**, God paints a picture for us of His original intention for the Earth. It is easy to see the garden of Eden as a prototype for what Heaven on Earth looks like. The beauty, the freedom, the freshness of creation. It is also easy to imagine because there were only two people and there wasn't a need for government, authority structures, or boundary lines. Later in scripture, we see another example in Solomon's reign as king, which you can read about in 1 **Kings 4:20-5:5**. Some of the aspects of his kingdom were:

- Abundance in resources **(4:20)**
- Personal prosperity for his people **(4:25)**
- Kingdom wealth **(4:26)**
- Governmental and organizational health **(4:27)**
- Excellence in Creativity and Arts **(4:32)**
- Knowledge and opportunities for resourcing **(4:33)**
- Favor with surrounding rulers and kings **(4:34)**
- Peace on all sides **(5:4)**

This sounds familiar, doesn't it? "Manifest your kingdom realm, and cause your every purpose to be fulfilled on Earth, just as it is fulfilled in heaven" **(Matthew 6:10)**. Peace, creativity, protection, health, favor, prosperity, and provision all sound like attributes of what God has in heaven and wants us His kids to have on Earth. What then? What happens when there is no pain, pride, struggle, torment, sickness, poverty, war, disease?

Some have been used by God to change history and culture by bringing these above attributes to Earth. Branch Rickey, William Wilberforce, and Abraham Lincoln and others have responded to their call in luxury -- Loren Cunningham, Bill Johnson, Benny Hinn, John Wimber. Many were fearless pioneers and trailblazers-- Martin Luther, John Wesley, Hudson Taylor. And there are still others whose names may not be written on Earth but are most definitely written in heaven. There is no one-size-fits-all model and thank God for it! Again we go back to the original invitation from Jesus, to be in the same way with Him. Location, persecution, and promotion are irrelevant. It is His face and love that is enough! Once His love washes over our hearts, minds, and bodies we lean into His words in John 13:

> "My dear friends, I only have a brief time left to be with you. And then you will search and long for Me. But I tell you what I told the Jewish leaders: you'll not be able to come where I am. "So I give you now a new commandment: Love each other just as much as I have loved you. For when you demonstrate the same love I have for you by

loving one another, everyone will know that you're My true followers."

John 13:33-35 (TPT)

With these words, Jesus gave us a new precedent. A precedent, in law, is a judgment or decision of a court that is cited in a subsequent or comparable dispute as an example to justify a decision on a similar case or point of law. Similarly, to a court of law, Jesus is using His life and love as a new standard of love for His disciples to use from this moment on and actually saying it is as you imitate Me that people will know who you represent. Or you could say it this way: Jesus' love and life is the standard of measurement for what love looks like.

Jesus flawlessly modeled love for every person in all the world to see. Even before being betrayed Jesus leaned into love so deeply that scripture says, He showed the full extent of His love **(John 13:1)**. We seek to follow His example and wholeheartedly love the world around us. He may ask us to go into scary places. He may ask us to stay in comfort. For some of us staying may be scarier and more difficult to obey than uprooting and following Him into the unknown. It's not about the going and doing, it's about the love we are being and becoming. Risk is relative but also required if we are to truly burn for Him all our days. If we don't allow ourselves to take risks and release the love and light of who God is inside of us, we will be miserable.

This is who we are: a company of revivalists who will be in the same way with Jesus, listening to His voice to make this Earth like heaven, the way Jesus designed it to be; revivalists who will make the name of the Lord great rather than our own; revivalists who will champion a greater reality rather than echo the current trends; lovers of God who know that Kingdom culture isn't a temporary assignment -- it's our destiny. This is why the phrase 'full-time ministry' is such a cliche! If you are a disciple of Christ, you are in full-time ministry. Your assignment determines where in society you get to represent Jesus: the healthcare industry, the entertainment industry, in government, church, family, or education. We practice our assignment daily by choosing to be aware of the heart of the Lord in each moment and simply doing what He says to see how far love will take us. So again, I propose the question: if revival was dependent on love, how close are we to seeing it? It is my prayer that your response now is, "It's here and I am on the move."

REVIVALIST BLESSING

I bless you in Jesus' Name to walk in the reality and the fullness of all you have learned and experienced in our time together. I bless you to run after God every day of your life and live in complete intimacy, surrender, and passion. I bless you to burn for all your days as this is what you were born for!

I bless you to be who God created you to be and never settle for less. I bless you with a spirit of boldness that would cause you to ignore the commentary of man and lean into the heart of heaven in your day-to-day pursuits. I bless you to be at peace within yourself, whether you are in obscurity or on a platform, that you would be true to your original design and honor both the Lord and His creation. I bless you in Jesus' name to receive the truth that God is with you, empowering you with the same anointing as Jesus who went around doing good works and healing all that came to Him!

I bless you to use honor and love as your weapons and to have the presence of God always be your North Star. The world is in need of who you are! I declare this generation, this moment, is ripe for your picking. Everywhere you turn there is someone to love, someone who needs a miracle, someone who is longing for the answers and the hope that you carry. I bless you to love with passion, live with zeal, work with excellence, laugh with an open mouth, learn with openness, lead with the presence, pray with faith, and give away what has been given to you so that Earth can be transformed into heaven!

I ask Lord Jesus, that you would protect your investment in your children and that it would always be a blessing to them and all who experience the gift of their life. I ask that You would be the only thing that satisfies them and that you would give them a heart to know you all their days.

In Jesus' name let it be so!!

THANKS

To my husband, you said the very thing that unlocked my pursuit -- "Who am I to stop you from winning the lotto?" Your love and support has meant the world to me! I'm a better woman because of you.

To my kids, you three are my dream come true! I love you all more than words can say. You are my favorite!

To my mom and dad, thank you for giving me grace to grow, for showing me a love that transforms, and for introducing me to Jesus.

To my sisters and brothers, God knew we needed each other! Here's to a legacy of laughs and doing life together!

To my best friend, before this became a book it was first hundreds of sweet conversations with you!

To my editor and dream instigator you made this happen and I wouldn't have wanted to do it without you!

To my mentors, heroes, friends, running mates, spiritual parents, and my teams past and present, all those who prayed with me, encouraged me, championed my growth, and put lighter fluid on my fire.

To the revivalists of the past and present, I honor you! Thank you for saying yes and teaching the next generations what it looks like to be in the same way with Jesus!

END NOTES

ENDNOTES

1. Brian Simmons - Translator of the Passion Translation Bible (Broadstreet Publishing Group LLC Copywrite 2017) -- **John 4:30** Although unnamed in the biblical account, church tradition identifies the Samaritan woman to be Photini. An internet search of her name will yield many interesting stories about her post-conversion ministry, including her being named as an "apostle" of Jesus and her eventual martyrdom. Regardless of the validity of the extra-biblical references, she will go down in history as the first New Testament evangelist to win a city to Christ.

2. Church this sentence is referencing the body of Christ, not the building or religious institution. Rutz, James. H. The Open Church: How to Bring Back the Exciting Life of the First Century Church. The Seedsowers, 1993.

3.http://eerdword.com/2019/03/29/turning-points-in-the-life-of-christian-women-kathryn-kuhlman/

4. Buckingham, Jaime. Daughter of Destiny. Bridge-Logos Publishers; Commemorative edition. July 1, 1999

5. Acts 17: 6 (NKJV), But when they did not find them, they dragged Jason and some brethren to the rulers of the city, crying out, "These who have turned the world upside down have come here too.

6. There is no Hebrew word for presence as in "the presence of God". The Hebrew word for "Presence" is face פָּנִים or panah is used to communicate in the Bible the presence of God but literally means His face. When we are in His presence we are experiencing Him face to face. (**Genesis 3:8**; Compare **Exodus 33:14 Exodus 33:15**, where the same Hebrew word is rendered "presence"). The Greek word in **John 1:1** In the beginning God was already there and before his face was his living expression.

7. If you feel blocked in your ability to connect with the Lord and hear His voice or if you have never experienced this kind of connection and you are interested it's super simple. This is what I would do:

- Renounce any lies you are believing about not being able to hear His voice. repent from saying that you can not.
- Declare the truth that it is your birthright and destiny to connect to the Lord's voice **(John 10:27)**.
- Invite the Lord to speak to you and ask Him to help you recognize it is Him.
- Trust that when you see things in your imagination, hear thoughts in your mind, dreams in the night, you are hearing from the Lord.
- Test the voice with the fruit test- does the fruit look like Jesus or the enemy.
- Practice what you are hearing by taking risks.
- Be more confident in the Lord's ability to speak to you than the enemy's ability to deceive you.
- Grow in your ability to identify His voice through reading books like Translating God by Shawn Bolz.

8. These things we don't know with our minds, we know in our hearts; we identify as we spend more time with God how He speaks to us and

how He teaches us revelation. It's different from knowledge. Revelation includes an experience and is given by the Spirit of God. **(Galatians 1:12)** Knowledge comes from the mind of man.

9. **Matthew 27: 46 (AMP)**

10. Rutz, James. H. The Open Church: How to Bring Back the Exciting Life of the First Century Church. The Seedsowers, 1993.

11. An impression is a thought, an inclination, an unction, a sudden sense of knowing which comes from the Spirit of God. It is often referred to as the still small voice of the Lord. Many people connect to the voice of the Lord in this way, however, it takes practice recognizing it is Him since the inner voice or "nudge" is easily dismissible. See 1 Kings 19:11-13

12. **1 Psalm 77:6**, a diligent search of truth

13. **Isaiah 58:11, Psalm 107:9**

14. I recommend Bill Johnson's excellent book on this entire subject entitled Strengthening Yourself in the Lord.

15. Shaw, S.B. The Great Revival in Wales. Jawbone Digital, 2012.

16.   https://www.biblegateway.com/passage/?search=Matthew+9& version=TPT Brian Simmons Footnotes- **Matthew 9:27** This phrase is an obvious messianic term. The blind men are hoping that Jesus is the Messiah who will come and restore sight to the blind. See **Isaiah 29:18**; **35:5-6**; **42:7**. Other than the wise men at Jesus' birth, these two blind men were the first to recognize Jesus as King.

ABOUT THE AUTHOR

Christina Andriese was born and raised in Southern California. Christina and her husband Ian live in Murrieta Ca, with their three incredible children- Aria, Ethan, and Luke. Christina loves to take any opportunity to connect with people's hearts and to encourage them to become the best version of themselves. Her dream is to see the church awaken to her full potential - to see humanity walk in freedom - ignited by hope, empowered to dream, and equipped to operate out of the resurrection power that Jesus provides! Years ago, she chose to become a student of God's love; now she lives daily to see how far love will take her. She is a pastor, author, and the founder of Revivallifestyle.org.

For more information and resources, visit:

RivivalLifestyle.org

Made in the USA
Middletown, DE
13 August 2020

15225864R00086